MW01256543

THERE AT THE END:

Voices from Final Exit Network

A Celebration of 20 Years

ANTHOLOGY EDITOR
Jim Van Buskirk

WITH FOREWORDS BY
Derek Humphry and Faye Girsh

This book is dedicated to Final Exit Network volunteers. Their unwavering dedication propels our mission forward, and their strength, compassion, and commitment inspire us every day.

Table of Contents

PREFACE

Since the first meeting of a group of dedicated volunteers two decades ago, Final Exit Network (FEN) has been driven by a clear and unwavering belief that mentally competent adults who suffer from a terminal illness, intractable physical pain, chronic or progressive physical disabilities, or who face loss of autonomy and selfhood through dementia have a basic human right to choose to end their lives when they judge their quality of life to be unacceptable. Our work is legal albeit complex, due to the challenges brought about by different state and federal laws. We proudly defend this practice for all who need it and support their loved ones throughout the journey.

This commemorative book is a chronicle of our organization's evolution, accomplishments, and the incredible people who have been a part of this remarkable story. It is a testament to the enduring spirit that has propelled us through triumphs and challenges. Within these pages, you will find a captivating narrative that reminds us that the right to control one's exit is powerful and affirming, and that comfort, support, and love at end of life are unique gifts for all present. Through firsthand accounts that have been edited for space and clarity, we invite you to immerse yourself in the rich tapestry of FEN's history.

The beauty of this book is that it is more than just a reflection on the past. It is an ode to a vision of the future. As we celebrate our twentieth anniversary, we do so with a renewed sense of purpose, eagerly anticipating the opportunities and challenges that lie ahead. This anniversary is not the culmination of our journey, but a stepping stone to new horizons where working toward death with dignity for all continues to be our guiding star.

To all of our volunteers, past and present; to our loyal members and donors; and to the families we serve, we extend our deepest appreciation. You are the heart of our story, the driving force behind our success, and the inspiration for our continued commitment to excellence.

As you turn the pages, we hope you share in our pride, our optimism, and our dedication to making the next twenty years even more extraordinary.

Thank you for being an integral part of our remarkable journey.

2023-24 FEN Board of Directors
Brian Ruder, President
Randee Laikind, Vice President
Anita Winsor, Treasurer
Janis Landis, Past President
Michael Klingler
Jay Schamberg
Gary Wederspahn

Final Exit Network Staff
Mary Ewert, Executive Director
Lowrey Brown, Exit Guide Program Director
Heike Sanford, Member Services Coordinator

Our Roots: Final Exit Network's Origin Story

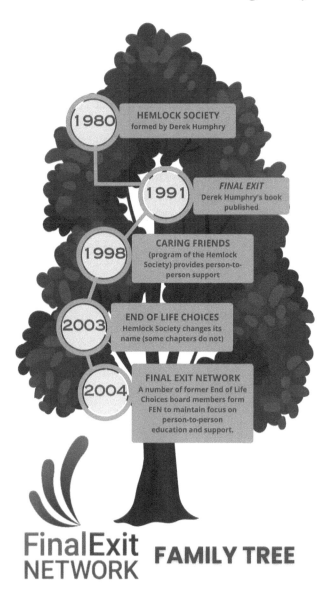

1980 — HEMLOCK SOCIETY formed by Derek Humphry

1991 — *FINAL EXIT* Derek Humphry's book published

1998 — CARING FRIENDS (program of the Hemlock Society) provides person-to-person support

2003 — END OF LIFE CHOICES Hemlock Society changes its name (some chapters do not)

2004 — FINAL EXIT NETWORK A number of former End of Life Choices board members form FEN to maintain focus on person-to-person education and support.

FinalExit NETWORK **FAMILY TREE**

FOREWORDS

"The Beginning" *by Derek Humphry, Final Exit Network co-founder*

My phone rang and my colleague Earl Wettstein said, "Derek, a group of us are planning to start a new organization because we don't like the way the Hemlock Society is now going. Will you join us, and can we use Final Exit as the name?"

That was in 2004, and this was good news to me.

Although I was no longer directly involved with the Hemlock Society, I disliked what I considered its retrograde, ultra-cautious policies under new management. It was agreed upon that the founding meeting of this new organization was to be the following weekend in Chicago and that this gathering of disenchanted Hemlock leaders and members would set out a policy of offering direct advice and guidance to terminally ill adults and those with degenerative illnesses. The new group would address ill persons in states that had no medical-assisted dying law or who fell through the many cracks in the stuttering legislation. They wanted to take advantage of the fame of my book to name the organization Final Exit Society. However, I successfully argued that a more modern name (which also reflects its national scope) would be Final Exit Network.

The founders all had substantial experience with advising on choices in dying, so FEN, as it became known, was quickly off and running. I was never in an executive position with FEN but, for the last twenty years, I have been a close adviser.

For example, when FEN ran into legal troubles in 2008-2009, I launched the Liberty Fund and raised $130,000 in ten days. Gifts came from all over the world, and the funds were used to help pay legal fees.

Today, FEN is a staffed, well-groomed, substantial organization—a credit to people like Dr. Larry Egbert, Ted Goodwin, Dr. Dick MacDonald, Faye Girsh, and others who patiently built it from the ground up.

*****

Derek Humphry founded the Hemlock Society in 1980 and was executive director until 1983. Self-proclaimed as "not a management person," he resigned to resume writing and public speaking. He is the author of ten books; his memoirs Jean's Way *and* Good Life, Good Death *are available on Amazon. This piece was written on July 19, 2023.*

"FEN: A Look Back" *by Faye Girsh, Final Exit Network co-founder*

1996: A big year for the Right To Die movement—and for me. The first legal assisted death occurred in the world, in the Northern Territory of Australia. The doctor was Philip Nitschke and the patient was Bob Dent, a Buddhist with terminal prostate cancer, who was accompanied by his wife, Judy. Also present was the law's originator, Marshall Perron, then-premier of the Northern Territory who resigned so the vote could be non-partisan. All three of the living people involved remain active advocates of our cause.

I met these pioneers later that year at a meeting of the World Federation of Right to Die (RTD) Societies. As the new president of the Hemlock Society USA, I presented developments in the Right To Die movement in the U.S. over the past two years—which were impressive:

- A small RTD organization, Compassion in Dying, had sprung up in Oregon after the defeat of their initiative—with support from Derek Humphry, president and founder of the Hemlock Society USA (the organization I was taking over). Its lawyer,

Kathryn Tucker, challenged the law in the state of Washington making it a criminal offense for doctors to medically end a patient's life. This was a challenging and difficult case which eventually wound up in the United States Court of Appeals for the Ninth Circuit with an en banc decision stating it was constitutional for a doctor to administer such medication.

- A parallel case in New York state involved Dr. Timothy Quill as one of the defendants; the lawyer was Lawrence Tribe, a distinguished professor at Harvard Law School.

The government appealed these verdicts in the Supreme Court. In January 1997, the vote of the Court was unanimous in overturning the lower courts' decisions. In July, there were five separate opinions. The majority opinion, written by Justice William Rehnquist, argued that it was up to the states to continue this very important discussion, but that it was not a constitutional right.

At this time, there were only two US-based Right to Die organizations: Hemlock and Compassion in Dying. Desperate people were calling us asking for help. Fortunately, we could recommend the book *Final Exit*.

While a do-it-yourself approach worked for some, it was clear that some of these sick people needed more than a book.

A dedicated group of us started asking, "Why couldn't we train our willing members to personally talk to these people and their families and tell them how they could die peacefully using the methods we knew would work?"

Our lawyer warned us not to consider such a plan, but I persisted, alongside Right to Die activists Lois Schafer, Dr. Dick MacDonald, and Mary Bennet. An American Civil Liberties Union volunteer attorney advised that if we did not provide the means to death or any physical assistance, we would not be doing the two acts that constituted Assisted Suicide, which was against the law. He reasoned that providing information and support was protected under the First Amendment.

That was what we needed to hear. We soon announced the Caring Friends program to our members. Although our services were free, checks of support came rolling in.

By 1998, we had trained twenty-eight Caring Friends—volunteers who were sent out in pairs to eligible members' homes. We made two visits: the first to educate and assess the situation, and the second, if the member desired, to attend their exit. Our Medical Advisory Committee examined medical records to assess each case. Eligibility was voted on by a doctor, a minister, and a social worker. Terminal illness was never a requirement, but unbearable suffering was. Volunteers were reimbursed for expenses and ready to travel throughout the country. Dr. MacDonald usually accompanied the pair when they returned for the second and final visit. Lois Schafer ran the program with compassion, tact, and efficiency, and Wye Hale-Rowe came on later, bringing helpful skills in family counseling.

By 2004, our board was getting anxious about our venture into some sort of civil disobedience. They demoted me, voted to change our name from Hemlock Society to End of Life Choices, and hired a new CEO whose specialty was mergers. It was announced in 2004 that Hemlock and Compassion in Dying were merging. The resulting name would be Compassion and Choices, and there was an early hint of conservatism in the laws they wanted to pass, as well as a hesitancy about our Caring Friends program. By 2005, the merger was underway, and I moved on.

These changes did not sit well with some of our thirty chapter leaders, while others felt that the Caring Friends program must continue. We had a meeting in Chicago to discuss next steps, and Derek Humphry offered his book's title as the name for this new organization. He gave a generous donation to get it started.

Final Exit Network was formed. Several people contributed to its formation, which is chronicled on the FEN website, www.finalexitnetwork.org. Although the name was changed from Caring Friends to Final Exit Network, the concept of home visits and trained volunteers, or exit guides, continues today. I'm proud that FEN continues to grow to help more people. It is a very successful response to the needs of desperate people and families.

STORIES

.

"The Right to Write Your Own Life's Story"
by Lowrey Brown

A growing number of us feel that, when the time is right for us, death should be comfortably in our own hands, not in the hands of doctors or lawyers, priests or politicians. We want to be able to end our own lives, in our homes, at a time of our choosing, without society getting its collective knickers in a twist that our considered, personal choice is somehow an affront to—and I stumble here—how things are *supposed* to be.

We are supposed to be living in small bands, hunting and gathering and dying long before the age of thirty. Let us dispense with fanciful imaginings of what is supposed to be and, instead, consider what makes sense. Let us also dispense with any romantic notion of a natural death. We have always done everything in our power to wrestle death from the hands of nature.

I had severe pneumonia as a newborn and was in an oxygen tent for days. That would have been my natural death. I took another stab at it in my twenties with a climbing accident that, without medical intervention, would have finished me.

Whatever road to death I take, it is way too late for it to be natural. At a less philosophical level, is either life or death natural if you have medications supporting your circulation? Or oxygen supplementing your breathing? A pacemaker guiding your heart? A caregiver spooning applesauce into your mouth because you no longer know how to feed yourself?

The vast majority of us come to a point of physical or mental debilitation that we never would have reached had we lived and died naturally. The additional time to live is a wonderful gift of modern medicine, but does it oblige us to suffer past the point of blessing, in indentured servitude to the medical establishment, to pay for that borrowed time? Must we then be cursed to endure exhausted, painful bodies or demented minds as some kind of penance?

Our lives are complex sagas with many plot twists, but they all must end. As anyone who has turned the final page of an engaging novel knows, the end matters. It matters deeply. No wonder, then, that so many of us want to be able to comfortably and safely end our own lives, on our own terms, without having to turn to professionals who determine if our personal values are worthy by their standards, or if our assessment of our life's remaining quality can be measured by their yardstick—or if our reasoning makes sense to them.

It is an unnecessary tragedy that those who want the option to end their lives must plan in secret, researching furtively behind closed doors, whispering goodbye only to their most trusted loved ones (if to anyone) for fear that their careful consideration of a reasoned, self-honoring choice might result in armed police arriving on their doorstep to haul them off to psychiatric incarceration—followed by the very future they wanted so desperately to avoid.

It is time for society to provide the tools and the legal protections to support those who want to choose when and how their lives end. It is time for society to create new rituals and new traditions. We need new understandings and a supportive social framework, not only for those who wish to consciously conclude their own lives, but also for those who love them.

It is time for proudly and openly planned self-deliverance. Let us make the preparation for life's end a time of coming together. A chosen death is an intimate opportunity to share and celebrate life's final chapter.

"The Coordinator is the Client's First Contact" *by Susie Y.*

Of all the important roles filled by volunteers for Final Exit Network, the regional coordinator is the first line of contact for all inquiries. When people contact FEN on the website or use the answering service, they can usually expect a call from a FEN regional coordinator within a day or two, thus beginning a unique relationship that may be fleeting—or may be long term.

In my role as a regional coordinator, my job is to listen discerningly, field questions, provide information, encourage, support, brainstorm, and try to help in any way I can. It's not for me to judge as I process personal stories from those who want to have control over a peaceful ending.

The reasons for making that first call to FEN are as varied as the people who initiate them. They usually involve chronic suffering or a recent, grim diagnosis. Some call on behalf of themselves, a spouse or partner, elderly parents or, occasionally, an adult child. Some are desperate for an immediate solution to their predicament; others just want information for "someday." Some are planners, and some have made no plans at all. But everyone wants to know their options.

Knowledge is power, and having autonomy over one's end of life takes foresight and planning. We are not a crisis organization and do not operate as such. As a regional coordinator, I listen carefully to people's stories. Often, it is obvious what they want, and we quickly get right into it. I go through the FEN protocol of what they need to do to initiate an application for service, which involves helping them figure out what paperwork to submit, followed by an interview with another FEN volunteer. Their paperwork is submitted to the Medical Evaluation Committee, which is composed of individuals with medical or mental health expertise who review the information and determine whether the applicant qualifies for provisional approval.

If approved, a senior guide is assigned to work with the client. While this sounds straightforward, the reality is that it can be a rigorous process that involves many phone calls and waiting weeks to pull everything together. Many callers are not seeking exit services. Some people just want to know more about FEN, learn how to become a member, or make a donation.

Others want to know how we can help someone diagnosed with early-stage dementia. There have been calls from people who are anxious about catching COVID-19; they often just want to talk and vent, and we share similar concerns. There are also worries about elderly parents who have "had enough." Some don't want to go through our protocol of collecting their medical records but would still like information.

Many callers are asking questions they don't want to ask and may have considerable anxiety around the answers. Regardless of the circumstances, I try to meet them where they are and do what I can to address their needs. I have talked to some of the nicest people as a regional coordinator. I may talk to some only once because that is all they need. Others call me periodically to check in with their health updates.

A few have even called to check in to see how I'm doing. Sometimes I have the opportunity to talk to spouses, siblings, adult children, and extended family. The regional coordinator and client develop an unusual relationship. It's not exactly a friendship and, yet it can be oddly much more than that. We may start out as strangers, but a unique bond is quickly formed. After all, we "met" at one of the most difficult times—when a person is vulnerable and asking for help in facing the hardest decisions ahead. Our conversations are profound as we explore heavy thoughts that can't be shared with just anyone.

Pretty much, without exception, I am thanked repeatedly for listening, talking, helping, and not judging. I care deeply about these callers; I think about them a lot and wish them well. Regional coordinators connect to callers through our shared humanity, and we extend our compassion at a most crucial time.

"Elder Rescue" *by Ann M.*

Some applicants may apply for exit guide services; others will not or cannot qualify. Perhaps they are too close to death or too infirm to carry out needed actions. Still, even these people may get valuable help from regional coordinators, directly or indirectly through their families.

Regional coordinators take great comfort in talking to these individuals and their families, helping them find a path through the maze of end of life decisions. Two such families I worked with illustrated that, even when it is too late for guide services, it may be just the right moment for other experienced guidance.

Francis, ninety-five, was a soft-spoken gentleman, quite ill, and unable to care for himself. He had lived an astonishing life as a professor, a husband, and a strong legal, cultural, and political advocate for Native American tribes.

Those days were now behind him. A widower confined to a wheelchair, he lived in a second-floor apartment with three shifts of caretakers, two of whom were extremely religious. He called FEN for help. He did not use a computer, had little to no privacy, and did not have a way to obtain the materials he needed without assistance.

I learned that Francis's good friends—a married couple—remained dependable and devoted to him but lived on the other side of the country. Francis asked the wife to call me, to see if we might come up with a solution. She was sympathetic to his plight and shared most of his views. Within ten days, she found a residential hospice that would accept him, with his doctor's recommendation. She flew across the country to his bedside and accompanied him by ambulance to the hospice, which had agreed that terminal sedation was an option as he had stopped eating and drinking two days before.

She remained with him for three more days, until he died peacefully, made comfortable with medications for sleep, pain, and anxiety. Francis was beyond sending medical records or applying for exit guide services, but he was relieved of his suffering through a generous and loving friend and Final Exit Network's problem solving.

Similar rescue came to a lovely woman who was dynamic and interesting at age ninety-seven. She swam daily until she had a bad fall, fracturing ribs and needing hospitalization for pain, trauma, and confusion. Sent from the hospital to rehab, she did not improve and constantly asked for help to die.

She had lived a full life and said she was "done." Her daughter called us to examine her options. She was moved to another adult daughter's home, where she voluntarily stopped eating and drinking, content with some control over her own death. Family members gathered at her bedside to assure her of their love, and others unable to travel Skyped with her, recalling funny stories from childhood and surrounding her with good humor, gratitude, and love.

She also had comfort care from hospice nurses and others. As she wished, her death came within a week in a nurturing and familiar setting.

These are just two cases of people who could not follow the FEN traditional path of applying for exit guide services but who were, nevertheless, helped by talking with FEN coordinators.

"How Did a Nice Girl Like You . . . ?" *by Judith H.*

People ask how I got involved as a volunteer with Final Exit Network.

My mother fell and broke her hip at age ninety-four. Though still lucid and making her own decisions, she leaned heavily on my opinions. The orthopedist told us that if Mom didn't have hip replacement surgery, she would be bedridden and uncomfortable for the rest of her days. Surgery would be her best shot at walking again. We consented.

Like many other elderly hip replacement candidates, Mom would never again be the same after surgery. The anesthesia and/or the trauma clouded her mind. Rehab failed to help her regain her balance. She couldn't understand why *they* wouldn't let her go back to her beloved sunny-yellow room in the assisted-living residence. Why did she have to stay in this smelly nursing home with crummy food and ugly wallpaper?

Seven months post-surgery, demented and miserable, she caught an upper-respiratory infection. Her assigned doctor prescribed antibiotics. When I asked why she wasn't yet ready for hospice care, the doctor said he had been waiting for me to ask. Mom was so agitated at that point that hospice prescribed a fentanyl patch. She turned her head away from food and water and slipped into a coma. Three days later, her spirit was freed to do whatever spirits do when they're finally released from their physical prisons.

I'll never know whether surgery was the right decision, or what might have been different if I had asked about hospice six months sooner. But I knew for sure that I didn't want to end up in Mom's situation. I'd heard of the Hemlock Society years earlier, so I googled it. That search led to Final Exit Network. I joined. In 2014, the newsletter announced a need and training opportunities for exit guides.

Because my travel radius is self-limiting, I've only had one chance so far to serve as an associate guide. That experience—a peaceful exit of a client holding hands with her husband and sister—convinced me that this work is for me. Our clients are such thoughtful, searching, reflective people. Serving as a phone coordinator allows me to provide them with the information and reassurance they need to walk the path to their chosen end. It is a privilege to be invited into their lives, however briefly. I hope I have their clarity and courage when my time comes to choose.

"Helping to Cross The Final Bridge" *by Jim Van Buskirk*

My involvement with Final Exit Network has been both a slippery slope and a crash course. It started when a regular attendee of the Death Cafe I co-facilitated for several years invited me to witness her exit. I barely knew about Final Exit Network but was mightily impressed with the expertise and patience of the guides. I immediately came home and joined FEN.

An article about my experience wound up on the cover of FEN's magazine, and the response was gratifying. Folks requested multiple copies, and I sent it to friends and colleagues in an effort to increase awareness of FEN services. In the midst of the attention, I contacted the lead coordinator, Ann Mandelstamm, with whom I began communicating regularly. At one point, she invited me to consider coming on board as a regional coordinator.

We met briefly in my backyard garden while she was in the Bay Area visiting family. Armed with a notebook filled with forms and guidelines and everything I'd need to know, she encouraged me to give it a try.

I realized the only way to determine whether this

was a good fit was to get my feet wet. I agreed to start by taking over Texas, Colorado, New Mexico, and Arizona, with the caveat that I could bail at any point. I was barely in the proverbial saddle when the messages started coming in—several at once. Before returning calls, I wanted time to hear the prospective client's story and explain FEN services. Suddenly, my schedule, which had felt fairly flexible, was full of demands. Of course, whenever I'd set aside forty-five minutes to phone a client, I reached their answering machine.

Initially, I was overwhelmed by the combination of time management, discretion (to the point of paranoia), and heartbreaking stories. I relied on Ann's support and encouragement. Over the course of many phone calls and emails, her humor and pragmatism were wonderfully grounding. "Lordy, Lordy. Arizona hasn't been so busy in months. Someone must have heard there's a new sheriff in town!"

In the first two days, I spoke with a nineteen-year-old with many ailments and no support system. Then with a forty-two-year-old fellow in Colorado, whose fortitude in recounting his heartbreaking situation had me in tears. A retired pharmacist in Colorado called on behalf of his best friend's wife suffering in the final stages of ALS.

A few days later, a ninety-two-year-old veteran sought support in Arizona. At the end of the call, her daughter expressed appreciation, saying she could see from her mother's face how much more comfortable she was having gathered initial information about FEN services. After the challenges of dealing with these disparate (and desperate) people, I could see the benefit in helping folks who have such little hope left. But I was concerned whether I was saying the right things and that the folks on the other end of the line were who they said they were.

Knowing about FEN's previous legal problems, I certainly didn't want to be the target, or cause, of any further entanglements. I was so green that I had to double-check with a fellow coordinator to make sure to whom prospective clients sent their applications. "Colorado" mailed his personal letter and medical records to me forthwith, causing my mentor Ann to quip, "Not only are you getting your feet wet, but I am betting you are damp up to your knees!"

Ann generously offered to be the interviewer, which simplified the next step. I can't emphasize enough her kindness and compassion, both for this neophyte and for prospective clients. When I read her report, I wept again. She had beautifully captured his untenable condition. Ann walked me through the steps of assembling his case file, which I sent to the chair of the Medical Evaluation Committee using a new encrypted email account specifically for this purpose. Success is sweet and sad in this situation; empathy is as much a liability as anything else.

In the midst of all this came a message from a member who was having trouble with the online procedure of having her employer match her membership dues. Since Ann was my go-to, she forwarded my query to FEN's office manager, who called to tell me how she had sorted out the situation. We had a long, convivial conversation, reinforcing my growing suspicion that FENers are a rare and brilliant breed.

Shortly after, I went through the same procedure with the woman in Arizona. I didn't realize how time-consuming it would be to assemble the personal letter, medical records, and interviewer's report, then scan them for the committee and keep the client apprised of each step. Eventually, her case was accepted for senior guide assignment.

In my first few weeks, I had successfully shepherded two appreciative clients through the process—a challenging trial by fire—and the pace, fortunately, diminished a little. Only now, months later, do I recognize a confidence and comfort level as I educate clients on their options for FEN services. I am connecting immediately, intimately, and intensely with people I would otherwise never encounter. Their profound gratitude for the work of FEN volunteers makes it all wonderfully rewarding.

"The Eyes Have It!" *by Deborah A.*

Throughout my life, I have had an acute awareness of mortality and our culture's death denial, in particular that of Western medicine.

There was the mangled birth, then welcomed death, of my first child in 1989, born with irreversible brain damage due to medical malpractice during labor and the fight my late husband and I had with the hospital to allow her to die. There was my husband's diagnosis of metastasized pancreatic cancer in 2000 and the insistence of oncologists that he endure brutal and futile chemotherapy until he had the courage to stop and receive hospice care in his final months.

There was my mother's unexpected suicide in 2013 at the age of eighty-six. Finally, in 2017, I developed eye diseases that greatly impacted the quality of my daily existence. I had to retire early from teaching undergraduate courses in the field of thanatology, the scientific study of death and the practices associated with it. After months of seeing local ophthalmologists who could not figure out what was going on, I found one who diagnosed pre-retinal fibrosis in both eyes. This condition made me see double—the world around me a complete distortion. Glaucoma in my left eye, diagnosed earlier and caused by a condition called pseudoexfoliation, required an arsenal of eye drops that only increased over time.

I entered a phase of life that required letting go of activities and identities in the world at large by redefining who I was as a person, someone not able to do and struggling to be. The eye specialists covered by my insurance were limited, with the best outside the network. My son, born fourteen months after the death of my daughter, moved to Colorado the week of my diagnosis to continue his glorious professional ascent. I was alone, and I had lost most of my vision.

I knew about Final Exit Network from my work, and in May 2018, I became a member. Soon, I applied for exit guide services. I was certain then—and am certain now—that I would not want to live should I go blind, an assertion I had made to my son and all my friends.

Also, while I threw myself into vision therapy to rewire my brain to see straight, I wanted reassurance that should therapy fail and if surgery was not an option, I could end my life peacefully with guidance from FEN.

Seemingly, within hours of reaching out to FEN, I

heard from what I have since learned is a coordinator. She was nonjudgmental, and I was impressed by her kindness. She told me to write a personal statement about my condition and why I was applying to the exit guide program and to get copies of my medical records from the doctors I had been seeing for the eye diseases. I sent these documents to her, and soon after, I had a phone interview with someone from the organization who was also kind and nonjudgmental.

My application was rejected by the Medical Evaluation Committee. I was more impressed with this outcome than disappointed. The fact of the matter was that I was able to drive with my left eye covered and a corrective lens for the right. It was not time to check out.

Four years and four eye surgeries later, I suffered from pain as a result of uncontrollable eye pressure. My left eye was eventually removed. But I am able to do and be in the world. What I am is a FEN coordinator for exit guide services, something I would not have been able to do had my application been accepted.

"Farewell, Brief Friend" *by Lowrey Brown*

It was Saturday morning and I was at the supermarket finishing my shopping before the beer and barbecue crowd flooded in for their weekend supplies. My phone rang and I pulled it out to see who I would be calling back later. Santa Barbara, California. I knew instantly who it was. I don't get telemarketer calls from there. I hesitated. For crying out loud, I was in the middle of the grocery store.

"Hello, this is Lowrey." His warm voice answered, "Lowrey, this is Dan ____."

Dan was calling to say goodbye. I had been his coordinator and, though he had been in the able hands of our exit guides since the Medical Evaluation Committee had accepted him for guide assignment, he had touched base once or twice as we had built a closeness through his application process. From the guides, I knew he was planning to exit on Sunday . . . tomorrow.

We chatted about his last few months, his process of reaching out to those he cared for, and of spending time with his wife and son. I had moved into the wine aisle, as it seemed to be quiet.

"Thank you for your support," he said.

"It was such a pleasure to get to know you. My heart will be with you tomorrow," I responded.

Did I really say something that generic to someone planning to end his life tomorrow? What was I supposed to say? What words could possibly carry what I wanted to convey? We hung up and I stood there, blinking back the upwelling of life and loss and something so much greater than the two of us and our improbable, brief relationship that started when he dialed Final Exit Network's 866 number many months ago.

Tomorrow, he would exit. He was ready. Today, the next thing on my list was hummus. Or had I gotten that already? I blinked again, trying to reconcile my scribbled list with my aching heart. They do go together, somehow, the sacred and the mundane. A young fellow considered which peanut butter to purchase; an older gentleman checked his list; a middle-aged woman, perhaps my age, moved distractedly to avoid the employee stocking shelves; and I pushed my cart slowly, the air thick with an unseen web of connections.

"Sharing a Final Exit Experience" *by Brian R.*

As Final Exit Network guides, we have many very poignant experiences being with people as they are preparing to die. Each experience is unique and makes us feel fortunate to be able to support people who have been enduring suffering and pain and want to manage their last days.

When we start our journey, we have some medical records and a letter of intent that support the reason for our visit. We have an address and a number of phone conversations as our connection. But, once we arrive, we step into a uniquely personal and intimate universe created over a lifetime. Nothing can really be determined before we cross that threshold.

*****

When we arrived, we noticed the house was filled with objects, both sacred and mundane. Grace sat in her big chair—now her only place—and, without any trepidation, reported that "today is the day and I want to go home."

Grace had lived the last ten years of her life in excruciating pain from a number of medical issues, including severe osteoporosis, that had resulted in a few of

41

her vertebrae cracking while she walked. Each day was a difficult struggle. Fortunately, she had two friends who provided moral and physical support through her trials and who were present at the exit.

Mary was a friend from the Native American community whom Grace introduced to her local Sufi group. They shared many Native American rituals, and a very deep friendship formed out of love and kindness. The other friend, Ann, was a nurse who had provided physical support but had also become a very deep personal friend, because that is how one related to Grace.

After we completed our formalities, Grace said she wanted to do a little drumming and chanting. Her room had a number of instruments, which she began to play, beginning by breathing into them with the sound of a soft breeze through an open window. She also sang with an unwavering voice as pure as crystal, a stark contrast to her failing body that could barely hold its own weight. It was beautiful and allowed us all to feel the energy build in the room.

After the drumming, Grace seated herself in her favorite chair to sing a song with all of us sitting closely by. "All I ask of you is to remember me as loving you," she said. She sang the entire song with a smile on her face so that we could all share her love and know she was prepared to die. She died peacefully over the next fifteen minutes.

What a gift it was to witness such peace and equanimity rooted in a greater sense of community and spirit, with the dignity and courage to approach death with ceremony and confidence—heartfelt, natural, and relaxed. It made us realize the importance of what we do and how fortunate we are to be able to do it.

"The Gift of Release" *by Anonymous*

As I peered through the kitchen door, I could see her sitting in her favorite chair in the family room. As I entered, gradually she attempted to stand. I told her to sit still; I would come to her. "No, I want to get a real hug from you."

This should have been telling. And if not, then the length and completeness of the hug should have alerted me to a change in today's schedule. I had thought that I was coming for a demonstration. It was just two days ago that she let me know that a friend of mine was also going to be there. I had encouraged her to meet with my Ayurvedic practitioner and Sun-Moon Dancer for advice with nutritional support and a potential pain reduction plan. When they met, it seemed that they had been connected in some other time. They had continued to see each other, more socially than professionally, over the past year.

She moved out of the hug and said, "I don't think this is going to be a demonstration. I woke up this morning in extreme pain and feeling miserable. I'm done. I'm ready. You don't have to stay if you are uncomfortable."

I was the one who had found FEN when my friend

seemed so close to crossing over sixteen months prior. She was in so much pain that even the simplest self-care seemed beyond her. This had been such a difficult time for someone who had always been active and involved in life. She was too ill to attend meetings, so I went to collect information, gather materials, and explain life-completion elements. I feared that she would lose so much of her abilities that she would be beyond the point of helping herself.

She had some reprieve in function and mobility, yet the chronic pain intensified as five, then seven, then nine vertebrae fractured and collapsed. Her greatest fear was becoming totally incapacitated and at the mercy of others.

I, like many of her friends, was grateful for the functional changes we observed. She and I talked about the confusion she was feeling with improved mobility, despite no significant change in her quality of life or her pain level. She spoke to me about feeling her connection with Spirit slipping away, so while I visited, we did more ceremony, drumming, and chanting. This would be uplifting at the moment, but as with many individuals with neurophysiological issues, it would wear her out for a number of days, and with fatigue and lack of distraction, the pain was most often unbearable.

So here we were, and the time had come for her leaving. The final dance began as the two of us helped her into her living room, which had become her ceremony room in the last few months. The senior guide and his assistant arrived, were greeted, and were ushered into the space. Introductions and some initial instructions were exchanged. These two individuals readily became part of our ceremonial circle, joining ours in this most auspicious occasion. My friend spoke of memories and elements completed. She played her drum and chanted the Sound Beings into this sacred space. Then she sang a Sufi song, asking us to remember her as loving us. Tears flowed as judgment was released and all that remained was love. It all seemed so easy, so gentle, and so final. She was at last at peace. We were very grateful for the work and wisdom of Final Exit Network.

"The Exit" *by Jerry Metz, MD*

Three adult children gather near—touching and holding and whispering assurances to a man who has lost his willingness to fight a battle he cannot win. Heaven knows he has suffered enough. Raw reality of his losses banishes dreams and denial; he will die, and he wishes to die now. The exit guides provide a compassionate presence, set an example, and are ready to offer a comment if the patient appears likely to make a mistake in the rhythm of his much-desired dance of death.

As if his physical suffering was not enough, minutes from the end, he is finally able to express a kind of suffering nobody expected to hear from his lips. "Is God going to be angry with me for doing this?" he asks, with tears flowing.

I am a senior guide, but I had never been asked this question. The children look up with puzzled expressions. It is clear this is a very religious family and they share their father's concern. What appeared to be smooth sailing has suddenly hit a rock. What to say? Whatever it is, it must run parallel to their faith, not across it. This is not the time to challenge others' religious beliefs.

"Remember," I say, "when Christ was on the cross. He cried out and asked God why he had been forsaken, and right after that, he cried out again and died immediately. You are a father and so am I, and I am sure if one of your children was caught in a terrifying situation and asked why you were doing nothing to help, you would move heaven and earth to get the kid and bring him home, right? Of course you would. And here we have an example set for us in Scripture, and we are all following that example. You have had all the suffering you can stand and you cried out for help. You've been heard. You're about to go home. God has no reason to be angry. So, go in peace, my friend."

He took a deep breath, let out a long sigh and, without comment, followed the steps and started the process that would end his life.

I don't pretend to know if he arrived anywhere—I deal in send-offs, not homecomings. I do know that his departure was peaceful. We should all be so fortunate.

*****

From my first call to Sara as a senior guide, I knew she was special and working with her would provide me with an exceptional experience.

She was ninety years old and had been a very active and successful artist. Sara was quite articulate, had a sense of humor, and was certain that she did not want to live the way she was being forced to at the time. She was wheelchair bound and required care twelve hours a day. She hated being dependent.

She told me that her children loved her and understood her desire to die rather than live this way. She asked me to contact her son, who was her healthcare surrogate. When I did, he said that the other three siblings wanted to participate. We scheduled a number of conference calls to discuss exactly what would happen and the timeframes for each step.

After three or four calls, we arrived at a date about two weeks out. When I confirmed with Sara, she was excited, although she wondered why the date was so far away. She had wanted to die for some time. On the day of her death, all of her children and a number of grandchildren came together in her daughter's home.

Two of the grandchildren flew in from out of town. They started the celebration around 1 p.m. They had fruits, cheeses, wine, cakes, and other food and drinks set out around the home. After eating a little, Sara retired to a small bedroom and, for the next three or four hours, all the family took turns spending time with her, remembering old times and saying goodbye.

When FEN arrived, I could sense the love and energy in the room. The children were all emotional but loved being together for this very solemn moment. The other guide and I joined in the discussions, meeting each person with hugs and appreciation. After forty-five minutes, we were told that Sara was ready to see us as she had just finished her last goodbye.

I told her how wonderful her family was and that she did not have to end her life today, as we could come back anytime. With her very strong eyes, she looked at me and said, "I have said all my goodbyes and don't want to do that again."

We performed the education piece of our service, and when everything was done, the entire family decided they wanted to be present when Sara passed. When Sara was comfortable, she looked at her family and said, "I love you," and she died in the next twenty minutes.

While there was crying and sadness, there was so much more love and happiness that Sara had died the way she wanted, and the family could be there to share the event. We recited a short poem the children had written, hugged, looked at each other, and knew we had just experienced something very special.

As I left the home, I knew that this was the way I wanted to die if I don't die naturally. I want time for my friends and family to think of what memories they want to share. I want to have toasts of champagne with cheeses and fruits. And I want everyone there to feel the love and energy that I experienced that night being with Sara and her family.

"Self-Deliverance and Bridge Traffic"
by Jim Van Buskirk

I first met Marilyn more than two years ago while holding open the side door of the Potrero Branch Public Library. The tiny woman was walking her dog down 20th Street and noticed my T-shirt, which read "Let's Talk About Death." What's going on here, she wanted to know. When I told her that we were about to convene a Death Cafe, she immediately asked if she could attend, and her little dog, too.

I have been co-hosting Death Cafes for more than two years, as well as reading voraciously, watching documentaries, and speaking to anyone and everyone about this taboo topic. Not that I consider myself an expert by any means, but as I become more comfortable, I am on a crusade to help others deal with their cultural discomfort about our common destination.

Perhaps that's why Marilyn invited me to accompany her on the next leg of her journey. A few weeks ago, she called to say she had contacted Final Exit Network and asked me if I would be there with her when the volunteers guided her through what they refer to as "self-deliverance." I immediately said yes, not knowing what this would entail or whether I was up to the task, and yet knowing that this was the next step in my learning curve. Marilyn was delighted and I was honored. And nervous.

I didn't know Marilyn well, but gradually learned that the eighty-eight-year-old had been a renowned Jungian therapist, author, and workshop leader. Still brilliant and brainy, she was intense, yet so soft-spoken that many Death Cafe attendees could barely hear her voice over the whir of the fans that kept the air circulating in the library's small meeting room. Over many months, Marilyn enthralled, educated, and perplexed many of us with her talk of patterns, the importance of this group in her life, and her frustration with her slowly diminishing capacities to drive, to see, and eventually—she feared—to think.

Astonishingly, she continued to attend regularly, even after moving from the Wisconsin Street house where she had lived for more than forty-five years to a senior community residence across the bay in Oakland. "I don't like it 'over there,'" she'd said, dismissively. "I hate that I have to go back to the other side."

"You make it sound like you're crossing the River

Styx," I teased her.

"I might as well be," she agreed, before getting herself to a Bay Area Rapid Transit station to return to her new living quarters.

After I agreed to witness Marilyn's departure, I spoke to Final Exit Network volunteers by phone. I was immediately calmed by their sense of purpose. They explained the process and assured me that self-deliverance was not illegal, quelling my anxiety about any legal liability. I didn't much like the term "self-deliverance," only slightly preferable to "suicide."

After several phone calls and emails, we had a plan and a date. I told a few friends what I was planning to do. One friend, a minister who had witnessed at least fifty suicides, many during the AIDS pandemic, offered helpful advice on what to expect. His counsel was invaluable. What a beautiful day, I noted, as I drove across the Bay Bridge.

Marilyn was simultaneously calm and keyed up as I entered her apartment. Taking a friend's advice, I had not parked in the facility's garage and only feigned signing in. Marilyn had originally offered to give me a sculpture by a well-known local artist, but I didn't feel comfortable being seen leaving her apartment carrying artwork. Instead, knowing I was a librarian and a writer, she handed me a box with the complete set of her published books.

Now, she was most concerned about a big wicker basket of cat food, treats, and toys. She'd managed to get her cat to its new home that very morning but had forgotten its food. I agreed to drop off the basket, assuring her I'd call the friend—one less thing for Marilyn to take care of. While we chatted, Marilyn was amused that she repeatedly forgot the word that came after "Final." When I supplied it for her, she remarked with a rueful smile, "Isn't it funny, that's the word that I can't remember?"

The FEN volunteers arrived precisely at 2:30 p.m., as planned, and I marveled at how patient, knowledgeable, and personable they both were. Because Marilyn could scarcely see, I read out the checklist of items, while Marilyn impatiently agreed to each one. She articulated why she was intent on self-deliverance, reiterated that she knew exactly what she was doing, and was eager to carry out her task. We watched as she signed the document with determination. The volunteers then showed her how to assemble the equipment she'd ordered, instructing her step by step. Despite her requests, they repeatedly declined to actually do anything for her, insisting that she accomplish each task herself. With persistence and a bit of frustration, she assembled the hood, taping the plastic tube inside and securing the bottom with a headband. She connected the other end of the tube to the regulator, which she'd screwed onto the canister. The volunteers emphasized that it might not be elegant, but it would be effective.

In the middle of the proceedings, the phone rang, and Marilyn, without thinking, answered it. The three of us rolled our eyes as we listened to one half of a very long-winded conversation involving $11, which Marilyn promised to put in an envelope tomorrow. "Don't let me answer the phone again," she requested, after hanging up. The poignancy of the fact that there would not be a "tomorrow" was not lost on any of us.

After Marilyn finished the sequence of tasks, she was asked again if she knew what would happen if she continued, if she wanted to change her mind, if she wanted to take a break. Adamantly: yes, no, and no. "Jim will be driving back across the bridge and there'll be traffic later."

I tried to explain that I was here for the duration and not to worry about my traffic, but she remained focused on the details, as well as the big picture. I was impressed and inspired by her resolve. Once she had decided where she wanted the event to take place—on a daybed with a sunny view of the bay—all was ready. After the brief demonstration, the volunteers explained that Marilyn would lose consciousness in about a minute and that the entire process would take less than fifteen minutes. Again, the three questions; again, the impatient reply. With no ceremony or final words, the three of us watched as Marilyn turned the dial, pulled down the hood, and began inhaling.

She closed her eyes as her breathing became shallow. One of the volunteers monitored her pulse. A few physical twitches, and soon she was gone. She looked peaceful. It was so sweet, simple, sad, and straightforward. I was moved by the simultaneously monumental and mundane moment we had witnessed.

After weeks of careful preparation, the entire process took less than two hours from start to finish. I drove across the bridge—no traffic—and immediately joined Final Exit Network.

"A Single Malt Celebration of Life and Death"
by Dick M.

Kate, an experienced volunteer with our program, called me and said, "Do you remember the woman we visited a few months ago in the wine valley? She was in touch today and said she had all her ducks in a row."

I remembered Ann, a member who had qualified for our support program. Although still in her early forties, she had an incurable neurological disease that had reduced her quality of life over the last two years. Diagnosed at twenty-four years old, Ann had managed the early limitations of the disease, working as a receptionist in a dental office. She had been an active outdoor person all through school, playing soccer and enjoying other sports, and had continued working until her late thirties. Then, the progression was rapid, limiting Ann's ability to walk.

With her disability affecting all aspects of her life, Ann found her close friends, even her family, seemingly unable to spend much time with her. Despite that, when we met her the first time, she had a cheerful attitude and was living, with some housekeeping assistance, on her own. She managed her wheelchair skillfully and drove her car with the aid of automatic features. Her only family was a brother, Peter, and his wife, Sue. When informed by Ann that she had been seeking information from a dying with dignity organization, Peter had been opposed to her wish to have the possibility of ending her own life.

After our first visit with Ann, we asked her to call Peter to see if he would speak with us. When he called, he had what is a common reaction to the idea that his sister might end her own life. Peter said, "Sue and I have talked about having Ann move in with us, and we're prepared to do everything we can to make her life more comfortable."

When I asked how Ann had responded to their kind offer, he informed me that she was adamant that she would not wish to do that, as Ann had told us. He said, "She has always been so independent. I wasn't too surprised at that."

After complimenting Peter for his wish to be supportive, I asked if he and Sue had seen Ann often in the past two years. He said they had visited once a year. I asked him if he would consider going to spend a few days with Ann so they might see how she was doing.

Peter and Sue said they would visit. He called a couple of months later saying they had just returned from a full week spent with Ann. He admitted they hadn't realized how much her disability had advanced and were now understanding her poor quality of life.

They were going to visit every two weeks to see how much they could help and, if she still wished to proceed with her exit plans, they would support her wish.

Now, some months after first asking our support program to accept her, Ann was ready. She was happy to tell us that Peter and Sue told her they wished to be with her when she died. When Kate and I arrived, Peter and Sue were with her, having wished to spend a few days enjoying some time reminiscing about their lives together as children, and since. They helped make the atmosphere of the next hours a celebration of Ann's life.

Ann was excited to tell us she had done something that was important to her. Usually, she had to limit any expenses. She wanted to celebrate this day by enjoying a beverage she usually couldn't afford. She had bought a bottle of Dalwhinnie, a tasty single malt Scotch that I had enjoyed. She, somewhat hesitantly, asked me if it would be alright to have a drink of it before she consumed the medication she planned to swallow to end her life.

I quickly assured Ann that it would be a fine way to celebrate and that we would love to toast her life with her.

Before long, Peter had unsealed the Scotch and we all sipped a few drams while having Ann tell us some of her memories of prior good times when she had savored the same drink. Her mood continued upbeat and humorous.

It wasn't long before Ann said she wished to proceed with her plan. She first expressed her gratitude to Kate and me for the advice in supporting her, and to Peter and Sue for making the last few weeks of her life so meaningful by being with her and understanding why she had chosen to end her life.

I suggested to Ann that Kate and I go outside to give her private time with Peter and Sue before she proceeded. She immediately said she felt they had been able to say all that they wished to over the past two days, and she didn't want any delay. She looked at Peter and Sue; they both nodded their agreement.

Ann was in her recliner chair, which she had told us earlier was where she had virtually lived for months, other than being in her wheelchair. She had Peter set the bowl containing the medication on a tray beside her. I went through a description of how the process would take place, to advise Peter and Sue of what to expect. Then I suggested to Ann that she have a small taste of the mixture she had prepared so she would not be surprised when she took tablespoons in rather quickly to consume all of it within two or three minutes.

Ann said, "I remember your warning that this would taste really bitter when we talked a while ago. So it won't be a big surprise. Will it be okay to have another small drink of Scotch after?"

I assured her that would be fine.

Ann dipped her spoon in the bowl and tasted the mixture on the tip of her tongue. She made an appropriate face as she said, "You're right! That is terrible. It tastes like shit." She paused only a second when she added, "But I'm going to get it all down, even if it kills me."

The deep silence was quickly broken by Ann's hysterical laughter that relieved the tension in the room as we all joined in the response to Ann's unintended humor. Peter fell off the arm of the sofa on which he was sitting, and he curled up on the floor with uncontrolled laughter.

After the hilarity in the room subsided, Ann calmly consumed the medicated mixture. With a sly smile she said, "May I now have that other drink?"

We all enjoyed the second taste of the Scotch perhaps more than the first, as it seemed Ann had helped us to join her in a more relaxed approach to the following minutes. Within five minutes, Ann suddenly stopped recalling a pleasant memory and her head fell back, gently asleep. Her last shallow breath was observed two hours later.

"Death Doulas" *by Jim M.*

"Hi, Jim, it's Wendy. You've got to help me die!" Her voice on the phone was determined. Wendy had been diagnosed with an incurable, degenerative disease several years back, and her health had slowly and steadily declined. Wendy had moved to Texas to be close to her sister Patty and had been placed in an assisted living facility, but it was not giving her the care she needed now that she was confined to a wheelchair and could barely feed herself.

I explained to her that the only viable option in her circumstances was Voluntarily Stopping Eating and Drinking (VSED). Wendy said Patty would never agree to VSED and that she controlled all of Wendy's finances. FEN's Guide to Preparing for VSED listed death doulas (now termed end of life doulas) as helpful resources, noting that the International End-of-Life Doula Association and the National End-of-Life Doula Alliance had online directories of members. I contacted Melissa from the National End-of-Life Doula Alliance, who spoke with Wendy and quickly established a rapport.

Melissa provided the name of an attorney so that we could make arrangements to obtain medical and financial powers of attorney to secure the care that Wendy needed. Fortunately, after Patty called me—and I explained Wendy's wishes and the VSED process—Patty had a change of heart and began fully supporting Wendy's end of life plans.

Melissa found a hospice service that was agreeable with VSED and arranged for hospice to interview Wendy at the assisted living facility. Wendy had severe problems with her short-term memory, and Melissa worked with Wendy to write down her health concerns to make sure she didn't forget anything during the interview.

Wendy qualified for hospice care and began receiving more appropriate drugs to treat her pain. Melissa had also investigated several smaller private care homes that would provide the attention Wendy needed. She met Wendy and Patty to tour the private facilities and even went back for a second visit to make sure Wendy was satisfied.

Melissa was in frequent contact with both Wendy and Patty to reassure them and answer questions every step of the way. She prepared a document clearly describing the VSED process and listed all the supplies Wendy would need to assist with VSED. Melissa also helped create a video recording of Wendy explaining why she wanted to pursue VSED and that she should not be given food or water after she began the process.

Wendy's health continued to decline, and her body began to shut down on its own without actually beginning VSED. A sign was placed on her door advising not to feed her, but Melissa still had to convince the visiting hospice service and private care home to stop giving her food and liquids. Wendy slipped into unconsciousness, and Melissa stayed and performed Reiki on her one night while Patty went home to rest.

Wendy passed away peacefully shortly before Melissa got there to spend another night with her. Melissa stayed with Patty until the funeral home arrived to take Wendy's body.

Melissa's services to Wendy, Patty, and me were invaluable. Without her assistance, Wendy would have suffered a much slower, more painful, and emotionally distressing death.

"Hold a Dying Friend's Hand" *by Laura K.*

My friend Judy had asked me to be by her side when she chose her final exit. She spent the next six months preparing and informing me of her plans. We discussed them at length and planned how I could be with her without assisting in her death. She had the book *Final Exit* and used that as her guide.

Judy had been suffering from chronic fatigue syndrome following the death of her adult son. She also was recovering from thyroid cancer and a divorce from the love of her life. She tried to heal with every method of treatment available and to sustain her lifestyle, with no success. She could no longer work due to the debilitating effects of chronic fatigue. She was going to lose her house.

She was estranged from much of her family. I went to every length I could to encourage her, suggesting alternative methods and diet, and I even suggested that she go to a Brazilian healer.

Judy chose to use helium as her means of departure. She purchased everything she would need and set it up on her bed, running a few trials without turning on the gas.

She wrote letters to all her friends and loved ones and had met with her lawyer. Judy was ready.

She died peacefully in her bed as planned, with me holding her hand. She went unconscious instantly. I made the mistake of not educating myself about the dying process, and I panicked when she lost consciousness because she still had a pulse and was exhaling loudly for about ten minutes.

I took a couple of runs to the bathroom, as my nerves were frayed. I feared she could be brain-dead and imagined the worst-case scenario of her being a vegetable in a hospital bed. Eventually, her organs shut down and all was quiet. I called a friend who lived nearby, and she came over immediately. I left a message for Judy's ex-husband, and he arrived a short time later. Judy had left instructions to call him after she died and that he was to call the coroner. The person at the coroner's office asked how he knew she was dead and said the former husband was not authorized to determine death; we needed to call 911.

We phoned 911 and were bombarded by first responders. As I sat in the living room, the police and firemen showed up, and I directed them to the bedroom, informing them that she had a do-not-resuscitate order. (I feared that they might attempt to resuscitate her.) I wanted to be upfront about being with Judy, and I told the police that I had been by her side when she died.

The three of us (friend, ex-husband, and myself) were asked if we would be willing to go down to the police station for questioning, and we all agreed. I did not have anything to hide and wanted to cooperate to alleviate any concerns. I knew I had taken every precaution to protect myself.

We were separated at the police station. I sat in a small room and was questioned intermittently for the next four hours. I was asked if they could take my phone, which they did. It was returned to me a few hours later. I reached my limit and was exhausted and told the investigator that I wanted to go home, and he gave me a ride.

Unbeknownst to me, my friend and Judy's ex had been released a couple of hours earlier. I called my neighbor and was debriefing with her when, about an hour later, the investigator showed up at my house around midnight to inform me that everything had been checked out and I was cleared.

What I learned from my choice to support Judy's decision is that I subjected myself to potential prosecution and accusations from family members and friends. It is with great relief that I can say that Judy's ex-husband was incredibly grateful to me. He understood her suffering and thanked me for being by her side. I am fortunate that others in her family did not decide to make accusations and that the police did not see a need to take this further.

With the help of [Derek Humphry's book] *Final Exit*, I did everything correctly to protect myself. I was able to give my friend her dying wish—not to be alone at her final exit. I miss Judy dearly, but I know she isn't suffering and that what she did was the right decision for her. It's too bad that we have to be so careful to simply be with someone who makes this decision to exit peacefully on their own terms. It makes what could be a loving, family affair a secret, clandestine event. Fortunately, there are FEN exit guides so that you're not alone, as Judy and I were.

"A FEN-Informed Death" *by Beverly Thorn*

For years, my husband insisted that he wanted a death with dignity, and for years, he researched options. He even had an underlined copy of *The Peaceful Pill Handbook* when I became involved with him more than two decades ago.

When he started noticing mild but concerning cognitive issues in 2003, he became heavily invested in learning his options for dying on his own terms. It was ten years before any abnormalities were detectable on an MRI or with neuropsych testing, and even thereafter, he functioned pretty well until 2016.

He was adamant about wanting to avoid being placed in nursing home care, and he certainly didn't want to end up being kept alive through useless medical interventions and spoon feeding, the way his own mother had been kept alive.

To gain my cooperation and support, Walt agreed that he would not take his life violently. He researched if any US states allow doctor-assisted dying for someone with dementia, especially if the person has clearly specified their wishes ahead of time.

He became a member of Dignitas in Switzerland, exploring options for qualifying for an assisted death prior to severe dementia. We joined Final Exit Network and applied for and received assistance from exit guides. I was astounded that two caring strangers would come to us with detailed information about nonviolently ending one's life with nitrogen, without any expectation or need for him to ever actually do so.

Ultimately, my husband decided that he wouldn't go off to Switzerland because he didn't want to leave his daughters that way. He also didn't want to use the FEN nitrogen method because it might cause legal problems for me or the girls if they knew about it. That left Voluntarily Stopping Eating and Drinking (VSED).

He talked to his physicians, who were theoretically supportive, and we talked to the kids, who understood. Together, we tightened up his advance care directive to indicate that by the time he entered a moderate stage of dementia, he would likely institute VSED. The booklet published by FEN on VSED was a valuable tool as I took on more of the responsibilities for facilitating his relatively peaceful death.

He ultimately did not act before losing the

necessary cognitive skills to stop eating and drinking. I think that he just didn't want to leave any shred of quality time on the table. But our advance care directive left very specific prohibitions regarding eating and drinking after the onset of moderate dementia.

Well into moderately severe dementia, as long as Walt showed interest in food and drink, we focused on pleasure eating only, forgetting about adequate nutrition and those blasted protein shakes!

We were to wait for his cues regarding waning interest in food. We were not to spoon-feed him. During the last year, he lost the ability to identify and use utensils properly and, in the last couple of months, he sometimes forgot the mechanics of eating.

Toward the end, he would sit with a small plate of prepared, cut-up finger food, and eat a bite or two, while also trying to chew the napkin, placemat, or cup. I dreaded the admonition that he not be spoon-fed if he indicated a desire for food but could not feed himself. To my relief, his interest in food and drink seemed to naturally wane, but with it came serious confusion, hallucinations, and agitation.

Had it not been for a close, long-term relationship

with his primary care physician, who spotted the need for hospice ahead of time and who directed all medical decisions based on the specifics in his living will, he would have spent his last days strapped to a gurney in the emergency department and transferred to a nursing home bed somewhere, alone and raving.

Instead, we were able to keep him at home, with a physician who was comfortable and willing to follow his directive to "keep me comfortable even if doing so hastens my death." He did not overdose, but he was able to let go of his fight and relax into death a few days after being sedated. It could have been so different, so much more horrible.

As his wife, I was one of the lucky—and informed—ones. I marvel at how easily he could have been sucked into the medical treadmill of useless and painful interventions, at how he could have died alone in agony.

But a thousand unseen angels were at work along this way, one of them being Final Exit Network. FEN does so much more than offer information about how to quickly terminate one's life. They offer knowledge, empowerment, support, and follow-up. For these and so many other things, I am grateful.

"It's All Divine"
by Jim Van Buskirk

I received a letter from a ninety-three-year-old woman who had read my article in the Final Exit Network newsletter about my experience being with a friend as she exited. Helga was inquiring about her own exit options. I called to tell her how to get information about FEN and immediately fell in love with her lilting German accent, mental acuity, and charming wit. She followed my suggestion and contacted FEN's California coordinator and called to let me know she was moving forward with her plans. We quickly became phone pals, calling one another every so often for a lively chat about her situation. But we talked about lots of other topics as well.

When I learned her case had been approved by FEN's Medical Evaluation Committee, I was happy for Helga and saddened I would lose a friend. Sensing she needed support with some nagging details, I offered to help find a home for a few of her most beloved German books. Although we had been phone friends for some time, I was even more impressed when I witnessed, firsthand, her fierce determination in the face of severe physical challenges. We spoke more frequently as she worked with the FEN guides to prepare. Helga was not one to ask for anything, but when I asked if she'd like me to attend her exit, she accepted gratefully. The frequency of our phone calls accelerated over the next few weeks, until the day arrived.

She embraced me at the door and promptly handed me a small canvas bag she had prepared, filled with final offerings. As we waited for the guides, we chatted about her experiences at workshops at the Esalen Institute starting in the late 1960s, and various other subjects. I was surprised, given the circumstances, how natural, and not awkward, our final time was together. When I asked how she was doing, she acknowledged that there was only one thing troubling her. The fact that carrying out her wishes had to be done so secretly made her sad and, she confessed, a little bit angry. She repeated her feelings to the guides, and we all nodded in agreement.

The time had come. We guided this beautiful and wise old woman onto her bed. As I looked at her, very present, limited only by her body, I saw her relief and happiness at finishing her life on her own terms. Spontaneously, she began reciting poetry—her own, she revealed shyly. As I held her hand, or more precisely allowed her to hold mine, I realized what an honor it was to be in this position. Whatever gift I might have thought I was giving, I was receiving multifold. A few minutes later she was gone, peacefully and painlessly.

When I got home, I opened the canvas bag. In it were books we'd discussed (copies of *The Peaceful Pill Handbook* and Derek Humphry's *Final Exit*), assorted articles, and a notebook of her poetry. As an example of her attention to detail and thoughtfulness, there was even a small Tupperware container of some imported cheeses she thought I'd like. I cut myself a morsel of cheese—it was delicious—and read through her composition book of handwritten poetry, some in English, some in German. I found the poem she'd recited and was filled anew with admiration:

At nights I pray
what I not say
cannot be heard
Oh Lord the sun is high
the sun that shines
is this divine?
I dare you better stay

a creature has no other way

to round this earth

in all its form

to kneel before the throne

you stumble thousand times

it's all divine

So let me pray oh Lord

to thy Glory

to thy will

when you are angry

I am still

Go kiss the earth

reach for the sun

reach for the moon

it's over too soon

the play is fine

it's all divine

I'd intended to allow Helga to have the last word and, in her own way, she did. Two weeks after the exit, the coordinator received an unanticipated package from Germany. She opened it to find three different kinds of German holiday cookies and a note from a man who identified himself as Helga's nephew. The coordinator reports, "He very discreetly said that his aunt asked him to send a few typical German holiday treats to me, which he was happy to do, and that he hoped I would enjoy them with a good cup of coffee or a cup of tea."

Needless to say, I teared up.

"Our Need for Agreement" *by Ann M.*

A woman calls Final Exit Network and asks to speak with someone to get information. In the ensuing phone conversations with the regional coordinator, her complicated family situation reveals itself. Desperately ill, she informs her coordinator that her family is deeply divided. For the most part, she has been estranged from her parents and siblings for years. She does not intend to inform them, or at least most of them, of her plans for exiting. With patience and time, the coordinator explains FEN policy and the necessity for revealing to close family members and friends her intentions to control her end of life. Eventually, this woman does not ask their permission; she asks them to respect her right to make choices for herself.

An important principle of FEN is that relationships with family members (comprising spouses, adult children, siblings, parents, and partners) and very close friends, plus anyone likely to know about the exit plans, are crucial to the success and security of the exit. The Guide Handbook says:

It is important that the guide inquires in some depth

into the family dynamics by asking probing questions about those who may not agree with the member's wishes. Although the member may not have volunteered their names initially, for the security of FEN's program, as well as its guides, we must know who, if any, are opposed to the member's plans for self-deliverance. Others may not be supportive but may have indicated that they will not in any way interfere with the plans. We need reassurance on that.

Over almost two decades of support programs in the United States, the only cases that have caused intervention by authorities have involved dissenting family individuals who were not aware of a planned death of a relative.

Final Exit Network has also discovered that this principle has a very important additional benefit. It brings families together in ways the members themselves may never have anticipated. This truth is at least as valuable to the family as security assurance is to the organization.

In the case of the woman at the beginning of this story, her siblings and parents, ultimately, all met before her exit and shared stories of the past, with plenty of resurrected affection and fond memories. Such a resolution did not happen easily or quickly, but some close family members were with her at the end, by mutual request.

Every death is sad to family and friends, but nothing is as painful and shocking to a family as a death for which they had no warning or chance to say goodbye. Since the court cases in Arizona and Georgia when the family policy was put into place, Final Exit Network has insisted on the informing of loved ones, family, and very close friends. Time has taught us that this policy is a healthy one, ultimately beneficial to all concerned.

In another situation, a very ill woman had two sons, one of whom was engaged to a young woman who had strong negative feelings about ending one's life. The ill member felt that her time was running out but hesitated to do something which might later cause her son trouble with his fiancée. She invited them to come for a visit, and she spent time exploring her options with her future daughter-in-law, being especially sensitive to her feelings and opinions.

After several visits, and with time to process the deeply personal conversations, the young woman made her peace with her future mother-in-law's decision. She even asked if the wedding could be moved up, so that her future mother-in-law could be present. They had a small, beautiful wedding, and family peace was preserved. A few weeks later, the ill woman exited with guides present, to whom she proudly showed the pictures of herself with her son and his bride. The member showed great emotional generosity and courage, as did the daughter-in-law, initially because FEN insisted on the sharing of information. What had previously been a tough hurdle became the source of family peace, unity, and mutual understanding.

As a coordinator, I have come to see the wisdom of this policy, a win-win that not only protects the safety of the guides and our organization, but also brings families closer together at a time of stress and loss. Wrestling with these family issues and facing them with tact, compassion, and discernment is worth the considerable effort that is sometimes involved.

"A FEN Experience Comes Full Circle" *by Shana M.*

In 2011, I was called to be a juror for a case in Phoenix regarding Final Exit Network. The trial lasted months, and at the end, the jury room was not a good place to be.

Some members of the jury felt very strongly about suicide, assisted or otherwise, and were unable to detach their personal beliefs from facts in front of them. While not a proponent of suicide by any means, I viewed FEN's process more as an issue of sharing knowledge. Then it becomes a personal choice.

In the end, we were able to acquit one FEN defendant. Then it got really bad. A juror (me) was seen crying in the hallway after the judge heard yelling from several members and declared a hung jury on the second defendant.

It was traumatic for me as a juror, and I cannot imagine what it was like for those directly involved. During the trial, I told my family members about Final Exit Network, and my mother seemed to take a special interest. But she was healthy, and I thought nothing of it.

Fast forward to 2018 when Papa Bob, the love of

my mother's life, started to decline due to heart issues and COPD. The last months of Bob's life were extremely painful for both him and my mother. He was in obvious physical distress, and she was having to watch him go in and out of hospitals, struggling to breathe, knowing that there was nothing she could do to ease his suffering.

After Bob passed, Mom admitted to becoming obsessed with controlling her own death and started attending local FEN chapter meetings. She was an amazing lady with great baking skills who thought it was fitting to bring her "Death by Chocolate" cake to the gatherings. Mom never applied to the exit guide program. She read up on self-deliverance and researched to do it herself.

She purchased a nitrogen tank and let the family know that when it was her time, she would not be entering hospitals or hospice. Instead, she would take her life at a time of her choosing. My family is Catholic, so this was a tough pill to swallow. But anyone who ever met my mother knows that she did everything with careful consideration. She told me that my uncle said to her, "I don't understand, but I know you and I love you, and I respect your wishes."

I must admit that I freaked out at first! Who wants their mother telling them she will be ending her life sometime in the future? But as time went by, she became more committed, having a necklace and jacket made that said, "My life, my death, my choice." I assumed it would be many years before I would need to deal with losing her. However, my mother, the most extraordinary person I ever met, exited on her own terms in her home when she was seventy-three.

She had developed severe allergies that affected her ability to breathe. But for all appearances, she seemed healthy. I think it was her emotional loss of Bob, not a physical challenge, that erased her quality of life. I learned afterward that Mom had cleaned out most of her house, with instructions to give what was left to those in need.

She had called her granddaughter, my oldest daughter, to let her know she was ready. She asked Ashley to phone at a designated time to make sure it had gone as planned. If there was no answer, she would call a neighbor. When the neighbor didn't answer, Ashley drove to the house, found my mother, and phoned me.

My daughter found Bob's picture turned toward the chair where Mom sat, so he was the last face she saw. A grief counselor went to the house, along with the authorities. She heard everything we said about my mother and said that she sounded like a spectacular lady who did things her way. We actually educated the counselor and a couple of others about Final Exit Network, though FEN was not involved in her death.

The selfish part of me wants more time. The selfish part of me wants to talk to my mother once more, hug her once more. But in my mind, I know there will always be another wish for "once more." I take great peace in knowing my mother thought about this in great detail, made the choice with a clear head, and was able to carry it out 100 percent the way she wanted.

My only regret about it all is that she was not able to have someone by her side due to Arizona law. We would have been there in her last moments, but even in her last days, she was concerned about others—true to form. The world is a little darker place without my mother in it, and I am going to aspire to make it brighter in her memory.

To any children of FEN members, I offer you this— nobody wants to think about losing a parent, or any loved one, for that matter. But the ultimate display of gratitude and love we can show them is accepting their wishes, even if they may not be ours. Our parents bring us into this world, love us, provide us with our foundations for everything, and we cannot ask for more. Tell them what you need to say now, apologize, forgive, and be okay knowing that it's not about you or anything you did or didn't do. It is a very hard personal choice and something to be honored—as I honor my mother today.

*****

Unknown to Shana, her mother, and her daughter, there is no law that prohibits someone from being present at a planned death in Arizona. When she heard that, Shana was shaken. She could have been with Mom. However, anyone present at a self-deliverance runs the risk of being falsely accused of assisting in the death, even experienced exit guides.

"FEN Makes the World a Better Place" *by Anonymous*

Let me begin by saying that I will always be grateful to FEN for being there at what was one of the most difficult times of my life, and that I respect and value the work that you are doing. It truly makes the world a better place.

Very early in his diagnosis, my husband had expressed a wish to end his life when his brain began to get really bad, and I promised to help him. It was the most difficult promise I have ever made.

From the first time I contacted FEN, I felt very comforted. I was no longer doing this entirely on my own; someone was going to help me figure out options. Everyone I spoke with was very compassionate. Just having someone else to talk to about it helped me tremendously, and I started sleeping better.

Once it was arranged that a guide would come, my husband and I were able to get more enjoyment from our time together.

The actual process of the exit was harder for me than I expected, but they talked me through it, supported me with love, and gave me a sense of a shared humanity.

The fact that two strangers would come in this very difficult moment and that I would feel such a connection with them restored my faith in the world when so many people are fighting and angry.

As difficult as this experience was, it would have been much more difficult without FEN. I am not a religious person, but I can truly say that your work is a blessing to the world. I will be forever grateful to everyone who helped me, and I wanted you to know what a big difference you made. In the time since my husband passed, I have been sad, but the reassurance of knowing that he ended his life exactly as he wished makes everything easier to accept.

"Shelly's Tragic Demise" *by Barry S.*

The ability to end your life as you wish is limited, and our personal right to determine the time, manner, and mode of passing is not ours to decide. Therefore, I have dedicated the rest of my life to helping those desiring the right to die on their terms to be able to do so.

Following three years of incorrect diagnoses, my wife, Shelly, was found to have Parkinson's disease. In speaking about the future, she repeatedly made me promise that I would not let her suffer. She neither wanted to wind up in a nursing home, staring at a wall, nor to live trapped in a world of fear and loneliness. I gave her my solemn word that I would never let that happen. Further, I told her if it was me, I would want the same.

She was my other half; she completed me, and she was my best friend. I intended to keep the promises we made. As time went by, she slipped further away mentally and physically. She reminded me time and again to not let her suffer and be in a world where she knew no one. Again, I promised her, without a moment of hesitation, to follow that promise.

Sadly, I will forever live with the knowledge that I

couldn't keep the promise I made to her. This is something that will haunt me forever.

She eventually needed medication. She fainted in a restaurant, and while it lasted less than a minute, one week later it happened again. She was hospitalized to determine the cause.

The next morning in the hospital, a young girl entered the room to say Shelly was being scheduled for a pacemaker. I thought she was in the wrong room, but the doctor told me it had to be done.

By 2010, we saw major changes in Shelly's condition. She was slower and her cognitive ability was slipping. We revisited our attorney to ensure that our advance directives were the latest and best.

I knew we were in trouble when my wife, who had been playing cards and mah-jongg five days a week for more than twenty years, suddenly started making mistakes. The women, who had been her friends all these years, were brutal to her and repeatedly chastised her for her mistakes. She often came home crying at the way she was treated.

I told her it was time to stop playing and we could spend our time together. She agreed. But as soon as that happened, virtually every friend of ours disappeared from our lives. We were isolated—no friends, no social life. Our best friends, with whom we often traveled and were with seven days a week, backed away from us. The wife of this couple—my wife's best friend—could not bear to lose her place in mah-jongg and deserted us. It was a very sad time.

Cognitive tests showed my wife was quickly drifting into dementia. It was clear that she was failing badly. I was falling apart as my wife had to be moved out of our bedroom into the guest room. My wife of fifty years was essentially gone from my life. She was breathing but no longer knew who I was and no longer recognized our children.

It was at this time I presented our homecare hospice unit with the advance directive and said, "Let her go!" That was her written wish and strong desire. In my mind, she was now gone, except for breathing. They refused, saying that from their medical perspective, she was not at the end. I was nearly insane with grief and total despair.

Believe it or not, several doctors told me if I wanted a quick demise to place her in a specific dementia facility because "this facility will kill her within days as it is ridden with contagious and fatal diseases." I put her in there.

It was a disgusting place. Fifty patients were in

chairs in front of a TV, and not one sound was heard. All were virtually dead, except for breathing. Several were on the floor. I watched in horror as not one nurse moved to put patients back in their chairs. I screamed at them, but no one answered.

By now, Shelly was frozen in one position, eyes open but without a gaze. In the last month, they brought a spoon to her mouth three times a day. "Why?" I asked. "It's the law," they said.

Shelly passed away June 6, 2014. They had tortured her for nearly four years. I have realized that I—we—must work every single day to get the United States to change its rules and allow people the right to die without any further explanation required beyond their specific instruction in their advance directives and living wills.

"A Good Death" *by Judy C.*

My mom, Lee Vizer, talked for years about wanting "a good death." Of course, we in her family teased her mercilessly about this. After all, death by choice is not your average topic of conversation. Besides, who else wears FEN buttons to the market, carries right to die flyers in her handbag "just in case the topic comes up," or lets people know at family gatherings, social situations, or casual bump-intos in the park that they can choose a humane death?

Thankfully, Mom laughed with great delight at all the good-natured teasing. We didn't know it would turn out that she meant it and that, in the end, she actually did have the strength and courage needed to walk all that talk and exit on her own terms.

Forty years ago, Lee's own mother, in terrible pain, desperately begged to die. Every day, my mother watched helplessly, knowing that legally she could not offer relief nor spare her mother this torture. She vowed then that her own end would be different.

Lee became a fighter for the right of those with terminal diagnoses to die with choice, compassion, and dignity. She studied, learned, and eventually became a passionate FEN board member and newsletter editor. Until the end, though, we were not sure that she could actually do what needed to be done to take her exit with intention.

She'd been diagnosed with Lewy body dementia, an especially terrible form of dementia with no cure, which ends in a cruel, miserable, prolonged death. With any dementia, the window for exit by choice—not too early when life is still good and not too late when one can no longer think straight—is critical and also tricky.

Amazingly, Mom timed her exit perfectly. As Lee reported, it's strange to "have no tomorrows," to remember she can eat dessert without worrying about getting fat, breaking in new shoes, or making plans for down the road. We weren't sure she had the courage to make "no tomorrows" a reality. And then she showed us just how much integrity and strength she really had.

She was calm, she was organized, she was content. She left with complete peace and unwavering certainty that this was best for her and her family. Did we support this action of hers? Well, how can you love someone and not support their wish to not suffer? Of course, we wished her death hadn't been necessary. But the alternative of living with Lewy body was truly horrendous, not something one would wish on any loved one, let alone someone like my mom who had been so clear for so long that she would not be able to bear that kind of ending.

So, yes, we loved Mom enough to support her in this wish. Though, of course, we miss her terribly. A good death. She got it, on her own terms. Lee's remaining family—big sister Gerry, identical twin Ellie, son Barry and wife Yvonne, and I—are left awed, full of admiration, and full of love. And we are so very grateful to FEN. You enabled my mom to exit in peace and comfort. There is no way to appropriately thank you for the enormity of that beautiful, kind gift.

"Why I Work for Final Exit" *by Eleanor A.*

No one really enjoys thinking or talking about death, but sometimes we're confronted with a situation in which we have no choice. Such was my introduction to death many years ago.

My beloved mother was diagnosed with ovarian cancer in 1971. At the time, she lived in Florida, and I lived with my husband and three little boys in New York state. Over the course of the next eleven months, I flew to Florida for four- or five-day visits, sat at her hospital bed, offered murmurs of denial and protestations of love. Conversations with her physician never approached reality because I didn't have the emotional strength and vocabulary to realistically deal with the situation. There were sentiments that should have been articulated, words of love and gratitude that should have been voiced. But they weren't.

The final months must have been torture for my mother, yet I never heard her complain. She bore each medical assault with grace and hope—or was it resignation? I'll never know. And, yes, I feel guilty.

When our beloved golden retriever was very elderly and infirm, I took her to the veterinarian who injected her with a barbiturate while I cradled her in my arms and sobbed uncontrollably. Princess had a peaceful death. How I wished that my wonderful mother could have died like that dog—cradled and comforted as a barbiturate ended her suffering. Today, I am a supporter of both Final Exit Network and Compassion and Choices. I believe in a person's right to self-deliverance, and I believe in legalization of Physician Aid in Dying. They go hand in hand.

So how did I become an activist? My husband and I moved to Schenectady, New York, in 2013, and I decided to put some muscle behind my longtime, but passive, support for the movement. I truly do not recall how I was put in touch with Hedi McKinley, but it was probably through FEN officers.

Hedi came to my home with bags of information, materials, and handouts. She was ninety-three years old at that time and a dynamo! There were other women who were supportive, helpful, and encouraging. Martha Schroeder and Nicole Sharpe educated me, and we launched a Final Exit Network Upstate New York affiliate. It was truly a group effort.

As a retired high school and college history teacher,

I found that speaking in front of groups was no problem. We reserved the library nearby and put an ad in the local paper. My husband, Jesse, helped with the technical problems as I put together a PowerPoint presentation. We printed hundreds of flyers and distributed them and...voila! Our first public program was standing room only! We had hoped for forty or so people and we had close to eighty. Yes, we got several to sign up and join Final Exit Network.

In the years since, I've done many programs in the area. I will travel to any venue. My husband always accompanies me, and we joke that he is my roadie in this endeavor. I always start my program by asking how many people expect to leave this earth alive. Haven't had a hand raised yet! It's my tribute to my mother. Her photograph graces my first slide. Princess is there, too, when I make the point that it would be more humane to let people die like a dog rather than endure needless suffering. Society evolves. It's time for the ultimate right—control over the terms of one's own death. This is truly the final civil right.

"Finding Hope in Something Hopeless" *by Kevin B.*

I am occasionally asked to talk with Final Exit Network clients or family members who have questions about religion or spirituality. They sometimes seek help in coming to terms with their faith traditions' opposition to self-deliverance. Usually, clients have already reconciled the apparent conflict for themselves, but a family member may be struggling to understand his or her decision and its consequences.

A few months ago, I had a conversation with a relatively young man who was planning his exit and was concerned for his mother. She was perhaps more religious than he was, but she was supportive of his decision and planned to be at his side every step of the way. A few months later, she called me to express her gratitude and to ask me about something her son had said before his death. He told her that planning his own exit gave him hope.

That didn't make sense to her because the whole reason for his self-deliverance was that there was no hope of recovering from his illness. What hope was he talking about? Hope is defined as "the feeling that what is wanted can be had." Most people who contact FEN would welcome a spontaneous recovery from their illnesses, but that's usually not what they're hoping for when they talk to me.

Their hope may have a religious aspect, such as the hope of an afterlife of some kind. There may be a certain amount of hope in knowing that the pain will end or the anticipated pain will not happen, although pain relief is rarely the main reason they choose self-deliverance. Much of life seems beyond our control, even when we are healthy. When facing an intolerable quality of life, choosing the time and manner of death gives us a sense of control. That sense of autonomy is the essence of hope.

When I was a hospice chaplain, I often advised my patients to plan their own funerals as a gift to their families. That advice was intended to prevent family members from fighting about "what Dad would have wanted." It turned out that planning their own funerals also gave patients a renewed sense of purpose that made their last days more enjoyable for everyone involved.

Ironically, preparing for their deaths gave them a reason to live, even in their last days. They wouldn't live longer, but they could live more intentionally—and that mattered. I shared these reflections with the young man's mother. She breathed a heavy sigh of relief and then said, "That makes sense, and it sounds like him. The doctors even used that word. They said his condition was hopeless. But they didn't know my son. I can see that by planning everything about his last days, he had a sense of purpose. He found hope in something hopeless."

"Goodbye—with Gratitude" *by Judith T.*

When the FEN coordinator called to tell me my application had been approved, she said, "Your only task now is to enjoy every moment." Yes! I've lived long enough with a great deal of pain, mostly from structural and nervous system problems, some of which I was born with and some that developed over my eight decades. Physical therapists and pain clinics taught me a lot, and I was a good patient. I kept moving, did all my exercises, practiced relaxation techniques and deep breathing, and made good use of hypnosis and visualization.

I worked despite migraines and crawling across floors when my back was in constant spasm. Also, I learned how to notice the world's beauty, even in intense pain. For the past seventeen years, I've been the one primarily responsible for my now 100-year-old mother. Mom hasn't been in much pain, but she's blind, bedbound, and unable to do almost anything for herself.

Her choice has been to keep living, and I've done what I can to provide for that choice. I've also known, very acutely, that her decision is far from mine. So when it became clear about a year ago that my chronic problems had gotten to the point where I could no longer do much of what I had been doing, I began to consider exit options. And when, a few months later, I was in an accident, followed by both a difficult recovery and a post-surgery syndrome that greatly added to my pain, I spent lots of time lying on the floor—the only spot and position I could tolerate, watching the pictures in my mind.

I didn't love the pain, but I did love how memories floated in and out, first illuminating my life and then letting go of it. Life and death. Two distinct states. And also not. The image I keep seeing is a fallen redwood tree, its apparently dead trunk teeming with life—lichen, insects, and so much more.

When a tree falls, more light beams through the forest canopy, allowing younger trees to grow more easily. Sometimes there's a "fairy ring," a whole new generation of trees sprouted from the roots of a cut or fallen redwood. The distinction between life and death—my little life and the flow of Life—is fainter and fainter, more and more mysterious. Now, less than two weeks before the exit I have planned, deep gratitude is my most consistent condition:

* Gratitude for FEN and the exit it shows me, which means I don't have to live years in severe pain and

limitation.

* Gratitude for the people in my life, beginning with my beautiful daughter and extending out to so many loved ones.

* Gratitude for the trees and flowers and sunlight and shadow I pass each day on my slow, slow walks.

* Gratitude for the work I've done, the places I've seen, the music I've loved, and the books and films that opened my eyes and my heart.

* Gratitude for all I know and can't comprehend.

* Gratitude even for the inevitable suffering and pain of being human, especially as we try to stand upright amidst the huge planetary grief we all share.

As I prepare for my last moments, I bow in gratitude for my life and in gratitude for my death.

*****

This piece was written shortly before Judith died in 2019 and is shared courtesy of her daughter.

"Nearing the End with Satisfaction" *by Anonymous*

I am pleased, as my death approaches, with this period of time before the end. No tubes connect me to pumps, or drips, or monitors. I'm in no pain. No real discomfort. No distress. I am continuing a loving time with my husband.

My death is forty-two days away.

In the meantime, I have the ultimate luxury of being vividly aware of who I am and of how I have lived my life. And what a luxury it is to have these final days with my husband without the distress of medical interventionism or pretended bravery, or attempts to soothe my dying body and mind. Now there is time, an aware time, to be certain our love, affection, appreciation, respect is spoken, is shown.

My partner regrets my decision, but understands. He's known since the beginning of our time together that when it comes to life, I value quality over quantity. Since my medical emergency, I've taken measures to address my medical condition, evaluating an ever-shifting paradigm of the new normal, giving careful thought to what I'm willing to live with, and arriving at the conclusion that I'm not willing to live with the degree of these changes.

This is not a stance out of line with how I've looked at life. I read Derek Humphry's book *Final Exit* in the early '90s and have maintained a health directive that I've updated every few years. I watched the decades-long decline of my parents, both in and out of hospitals with cardiac and stroke issues, which solidified my determination to do my best to not let that happen to me.

Since the crisis, I've received excellent and caring medical attention that has included countless tests and difficult periods of adjusting medications to address side effects. My condition has resulted in considerable loss of strength and endurance.

This loss of strength has eliminated a major part of my life: independent travel. For about three decades, I traveled independently for at least two or three months a year, much of it in Africa and Asia, where travel can be somewhat demanding.

I've been preparing for the end of my life by disposing of many possessions. I did not find this process to be painful but enjoyed revisiting these reminders of the fullness of my life. This disposition was all in an effort toward easing the transition for my husband, who is a caring, loving man and has actively and willingly adjusted our patterns of living to accommodate the changes my illnesses have brought about.

This decision is not born out of need. I have the good fortune to possess the personal, financial, and insurance resources to live a longer life. But I am greatly diminished and not willing to continue living in this state of being. And there is no hope for improvement. I have no fear of death. I know this life is it, that my legacy is in the hearts and minds of those I've loved, have known. I'm satisfied that, overall, my impact has been more positive than negative.

I know there are those who will not understand why I have chosen this path, and I'm certainly not advocating it for everyone. But I am so grateful that, if fate permits, we have the choice to not experience a slow, debilitating decline and that I'm able to enjoy my life until the end.

"Stepping Away" *by Myriam Coppens*

This is my retirement letter, something I have been thinking about for some time. It is with deep gratitude that I am writing to all of you, some I have known for years, some I have known for a while, and some I have crossed paths with. Wonderful people!

I would like to share my last face-to-face case with you, as a senior guide. I had the amazing privilege to be present and witness a great love. It was a while ago that I met this sweet couple. They lived in a tiny, brightly decorated, neat little home.

He presented as a striking figure, a tall, attractive man, diagnosed with early Alzheimer's. A former biker. She was a beautiful, petite woman. They had found each other some time ago when they both immediately recognized each other as soul mates.

They were deeply in love with each other, experiencing great pleasure in each other's company. She told me she gladly would take care of him as his disease overtook him. But he clearly did not want this. Instead, he wished to go before declining further. It was time to go, however painful that was for both.

He was ready during the first visit, but she had no support person present with her. We scheduled another visit when an old friend of theirs could come and be a support to both, but mostly for her after his death. Two weeks later, I joined them again. When it was time for him to lie down, I suggested they say goodbye one last time.

Both hugged. He held her tight to his body, cupping her close to him, while she stood on her toes, both kissing through their masks. I suggested they remove their masks, and they kissed one last time. Such love and pain all in this one last kiss.

He died being held by her, this tiny loving woman curled up against his side, waves of grief racking her body and heart. He died a big man held by love.

Thank you! Thank you! I wish you well. Keep doing this very important work. You are all amazing!

*****

Myriam Coppens was a quiet, unassuming giant of the Right To Die movement for more than thirty years, and she blessed FEN as an exit guide since 2008. She started the Portland Hemlock Society in 1989, testified for Oregon's seminal Death With Dignity law, and labored tirelessly as an advocate for end of life choice. She worked passionately with countless FEN clients whom she supported in achieving a peaceful, dignified death.

"Myriam was the first guide I worked with, and she took me under her wing as I learned the ropes. I remember one visit watching her calmly navigate some very intense family dynamics. I navigated that visit with eyes wide and mouth closed. There was no one better to teach me that guiding is a lot more than tanks and tubing." —Lowrey Brown, FEN Client Services Director

"Juanita's Spirituality" *by Kevin B.*

I met Juanita during exit guide training in 2016. Shortly after the training, she asked me to serve as an associate guide for a client who requested spiritual support. The situation required us to stay in the client's area for two days, during which time I learned a bit about Juanita's career as a psychologist, her sons, her art and, of course, her passion for FEN. I felt privileged to be given a glimpse into her remarkable life. A while later, she asked if I could provide spiritual counseling for another client over the phone, even if I didn't act in a guide capacity. The client was so grateful that Juanita recommended my services to all guides, and I soon found myself having phone consultations with clients across the country. Those phone consultations have also indirectly led to the board considering developing post-exit debriefings for guides, both as emotional/spiritual support and as a means for continual improvement of our guide program.

Juanita's stated reason for inviting me to go on that first exit trip with her was that she didn't feel qualified to provide spiritual guidance. I can't help but smile at that comment now. Maybe she didn't have the vocabulary to be comfortable discussing certain religions, but I think living a spiritual life is ultimately about service and being fully present, the combination of which, in turn, requires equal parts grace, courage, and humility. Juanita clearly lived a life of service, and anyone who knew her would say she was fully present.

I am optimistic that her suggestion to offer spiritual support to clients and guides will lead to an even stronger guide program. It is difficult to imagine a greater legacy. I don't think I've ever known anyone more spiritual on so many levels.

*****

Juanita was an accomplished artist and a staunch advocate of death with dignity. This was written following her death in 2018.

"A Conversation with Fran Schindler" *by Michael J.*

Senior guide Fran Schindler's voice was raspy after five days of protesting in Washington, DC, but this remarkable seventy-nine-year-old's enthusiasm for FEN, and life in general, was loud and clear. "The privilege of someone being willing to have me with them when they die, when I only just sit with them, is the most meaningful thing I have ever done."

In the late 1980s, Fran faced a series of daunting issues: a brain tumor, divorce, and mysterious symptoms which mimicked ALS. She acknowledges that she became obsessed with finding ways to kill herself during those dark days. Eventually, she heard Faye Girsh's lecture about FEN. She quickly signed up for training and got her FEN membership card in November 2006. Twelve years later, she estimates she's been present for more than seventy individuals who have taken their lives using FEN protocol.

"At the FEN training class, I discovered a major benefit of being a FEN member. I looked at the trainers and my fellow classmates—people who didn't know me—and realized that if I needed them, they would be there for me. It gave me such peace of mind that my obsession with finding a way to die gradually went away."

Asked about unusual experiences, Fran recalled the time she and a fellow guide had to wait forty-five minutes in a bus stop shelter until the client's guest left the premises. "Bus drivers kept stopping and several commented on what a cute couple we were. It was pretty funny."

Fran asks clients to use the phrase, "I will get dead." Fran explained she started using this phrase to ensure clients give informed consent.

When she asked one of her first clients, "What's going to happen to you [when you use our protocol]?" The client responded, "I'm going to live." When asked to clarify, the client said her spirit was going to live forever.

At that point, Fran realized the importance of getting informed consent and improvised what has become her signature approach. "Getting dead is not an emergency. Clients must give informed consent. So at the first visit and every visit, I ask them, 'What is going to happen to this physical body when you pull the hood down?' And they must say, 'I will get dead.' That tells me that they know that dead is dead."

A retired psychiatric nurse with three adult children

and two grandkids, Fran still finds time for art and participating in political protests, in addition to her FEN activities. With her usual flair for creativity, Fran turned the handcuffs used on her during a recent protest into a piece of found art.

Fran's advice to others? "Start doing what you want and don't put it off. People say they want to find meaning in their lives. I say, you have to live a meaningful life before you can find meaning in your life."

Sage advice from a very wise woman.

"Chambers Wears Many FEN Hats" *by Jay Niver*

Lily Chambers has a career and résumé so varied that you would not be surprised if she fixed your laptop, repaired your car, and grilled succulent barbecue while coaching her clients in myriad ways.

She joined FEN a few years ago after learning of us via a family friend who was involved in a planned death. FEN's mission and work captivated her, but Lily had long been drawn to end of life issues through Grandma Carol.

"My grandmother belonged to the Hemlock Society, and she was very 'death positive,'" Lily said. The friend involved in the exit had also been Carol's caretaker. Lily didn't intend to embrace death with dignity and the right to die, but after learning of FEN and the exit guide program, she went through guide training.

"It felt like a 'big click' for me that the people who are coming to FEN really need help," she explained. "To fill that role is one of the most interesting and valuable things anyone could do."

Helping others is what Lily does in her work as a personal coach, specializing in areas like grief, energy healing, and working with artists.

In another era, a coach taught kids how to dribble, pass, or hit a golf ball, but coaching has become a full-time field for specially trained advisers who help people through all kinds of life challenges.

Lily's varied expertise transfers easily to FEN. Besides being an end of life doula and former hospice volunteer, her interpersonal skills have let her mesh easily with FEN staff, volunteers, and other contractors on a number of levels.

After knowing of her interest in the exit guide program, FEN Executive Director Mary Ewert asked Lily if she would contribute in other ways. Her response was an enthusiastic "yes."

She started gently with some data entry, then assumed the job of producing FEN's online Right To Die News, the periodic collection of worldwide news emailed to subscribers. Sifting through end of life stories from around the globe "opened my eyes to so many related issues," she said.

Now, she's also organizing and providing technical support for the Chosen Death Forum, the monthly online Zoom, and working with past FEN President Janis Landis on curriculum for end of life doulas as FEN partners with them to improve training in their field.

When not coaching clients or helping FEN, Lily has long been involved in providing space for a variety of community arts pursuits, and she's also a performing artist.

"Ann Mandelstamm Found Her Tribe" *by Jay Niver*

Ann Mandelstamm was never a pariah. The longtime FEN coordinator for exit guide services was not unlikeable and was hardly offensive. She'd been a high school English teacher for thirty-five years, had plenty of friends, was well respected, and raised three great kids.

Still, she says, something was missing. "I felt pretty comfortable, but I never quite fit in anyplace I was in life."

That changed after she retired, when her children were grown and successful on their own. "I've always needed meaning and purpose in life," Ann says. "When I was teaching and raising children, I had meaning and purpose out the wazoo. But once I retired, I was lost. I wasn't going to have a whole new career, and I certainly wasn't going to have any more babies."

Final Exit Network became her baby, and she confessed as much at a FEN Chicago meeting. As Ann recalls, volunteers were informally sharing what they thought were the best (and worst) things about the organization. When it came to her, she blurted it out: "The best thing is, I found my tribe! People laugh at me because I say this, but it's true. Here's my tribe. I found it! I love it.

I love the people in Final Exit Network, even the ones I tangle with once in a while."

Ann's affinity for the right to die began when she was a young adult. She explains: "I noticed my parents' friends, in their sixties and seventies, and many of them had cancer. They would go through these terrible things, surgeries, chemo, radiation . . . and some of them did recover. But then, if they lived into their eighties and nineties, many of them developed dementia.

"So after all that suffering and medical care, they ended up mostly in nursing homes, not knowing where they were and what they were doing. These were really fine, well educated, sharp people, and it ended up so badly. It made me feel like, 'There's something wrong with this.'"

That's not for Ann.

"If I ever get some kind of fatal illness, I'm not ending my days in a wheelchair in a hospital basement waiting for some more chemo," she says. Ann, eighty-two, is nowhere near that point, but admits, "I'm getting older, and my memory is not as great. I'm worried about maybe forgetting something important because there are so many, many pieces about being a coordinator, and you can't let any of them drop."

Ann has coordinated more than 100 clients who were approved. More importantly, she says, "There are thousands of people I've talked to" in the last seven years. Many never applied for exit services, but recruiting is not what FEN coordinators are about. "It's so valuable to sit and talk with them, to educate and answer their questions about VSED or anything else," Ann explains. "This has been a godsend for me. I feel so lucky because FEN just gave me so much in my life."

Others would say the same thing about Ann Mandelstamm.

"A Tribute to Tom Tuxill" *by Carol B.*

On November 3, 2021, with the guidance and support of an End of Life Washington exit guide—and in the presence of his son; daughter; and partner, Sue—Tom Tuxill died. He had been diagnosed with terminal brain lymphoma in September.

Tom's death marks the end of a life lived with enthusiasm and compassion. We, in FEN, who had the privilege of volunteering with Tom, learned and benefited in countless ways from his wisdom and commitment.

My own career as a FEN volunteer began in 2016 when I joined the Medical Evaluation Committee (MEC), which Tom had chaired for the previous five years.

At his suggestion, I became MEC chair in January 2018. Tom told me I would have his undying gratitude if I would consider taking over the role. I will always be grateful to him for the steadfast support, astute guidance, and warm friendship he gave me in the years that followed.

Tom became interested in the right to die when he was diagnosed with systemic large-cell lymphoma in 1997. He retired as an ophthalmologist and underwent intensive treatment over the years when the disease recurred. Given the poor long-term prognosis, it behooved him to educate himself about peaceful methods of self-deliverance.

Tom began with FEN in 2010. He was truly a volunteer extraordinaire, serving not only as MEC chair for six years, but also as a senior guide for seven years, board member for eight years, and senior medical adviser. Finally, he was an invaluable member of numerous committees. His tireless right to die advocacy shines as a bright light for those of us who will continue this work in his memory.

In our last conversation, Tom spoke about the peace of mind he felt, having provided a compassionate presence at the deaths of clients, and having learned what to expect, and what his family might expect, at his own exit.

It was Tom's nature to pursue interests passionately, and FEN benefited hugely from this trait. However, FEN wasn't the only recipient of Tom's dedication. He also loved family and friends, fishing, flying, and football. He had an appetite for life and adventure. His life illustrates so beautifully how preparing ourselves for death frees us to embrace life more openly.

I will miss Tom deeply. At the same time, I find comfort and inspiration in the story of his life and death. Tom's strengths as a fellow volunteer and friend were legion, and it's impossible to put into words the quality of our conversations over the years. He was unfailingly generous and patient, and he always seemed to have time to engage and lend support and guidance.

He never made me feel like I was interrupting, despite my myriad calls about MEC issues. His calm, gracious problem-solving approach, combined with the depth of his experience and knowledge, were invaluable. I always ended our conversations feeling encouraged and glad I had phoned.

Tom was an inspirational person for me and for all of us who had the privilege of knowing him. He made us all better people.

FEN President Brian Ruder wrote the following in a memory book FEN volunteers compiled for Tom before he died:

"Tom, you are, and always have been, my guiding light when it comes to FEN. Your compassion for the clients and the volunteers has helped me keep things in perspective. Your great desire to find the best in everyone is something special that I have always envied. You are the best volunteer that FEN has ever had. Your dedication and support to our organization is the foundation of our changing culture. I appreciate all of your support, especially when it was a hard choice. I will remember you as one of the best I have ever had the opportunity to work with. Thank you."

"Exit Right: A Wisconsin Love Story" *by Anonymous*

Faced with ever-greater losses of mental capacity and increasing suffering and pain, Mary and I have decided individually, and together, to end our lives. To go together as one heart, one soul, one love. On Thursday, January 7, 2021, we hastened our deaths. By our choice, we died gently and peacefully while holding hands and lying side-by-side in our bed at home.

For us, it was the culmination of our fifty-five-plus years of love and life together in which we had become one life, one heart, one soul. A grand finale for our lives lived fully together, our cup running over. We emphasize that we see this also as the beginning of a new life together, one which we cannot define, but which we know in our heart of hearts to be a life of new freedom, innocence, beauty, love, and peace. So begins our new grand adventure.

Mary was diagnosed with dementia in early summer of 2020. We had suspected its presence in her for several years. We intentionally delayed a medical diagnosis because there seemed no cure beyond what we were already doing and because we knew the definitive diagnosis would only give us more fear and dread. Her symptoms have steadily worsened, especially since summer.

I was diagnosed with rheumatoid arthritis over ten years ago. For years before, I could find no diagnosis for my joint pain in my neck, shoulders, back, wrists, and knees. Finally, I found one and have had excellent medical care since. Yet, for me, the chronic pain has been challenging and has had a cumulative effect, slowly stealing away the zest, passion, and wild desire for life that I have loved in myself and hope you have known in me.

I still experience much pain. I have long been dependent on opioids and other drugs for any sense of well-being. I must use more and more of these drugs just to get through the day and night. These are not complaints. Hardly so. Mary and I have long celebrated our lives and have been filled with gratitude for our life together with all of you all these years. The vision that we might go together has seemed a promise and a crescendo.

We have approached our deaths just as we have tried to live each day—with an ever wider and deeper appreciation of the beauty all around us, with an ever greater sense of the sacredness of our lives and yours, with profound reverence for all persons and creatures and moments, and for creation itself. With deepest discernment and personal authenticity, we feel we have been called to this graceful ending together. At age eighty-two, we share a sense of wholeness and completion which younger people cannot yet grasp. This fullness slowly and generously has come upon us and has offered this right time.

We are deeply certain that this ending also is a new beginning for us, a transformation into a life even more expansive and beautiful. Nothing will be lost; all will be gained. We look forward to a more relaxing and profound, if inexplicable, intimacy with each other, with this world and with you. Everywhere in nature, life and death are so intimately intertwined. In the dark underground, a seed husk breaks open into a shoot, then reaches upward to find the light and warmth of the sun. This forms a stem, then stalk or trunk, then branch, then twig, then leaf, then fruit, then new seed.

The seed drops into soil made rich and nurturing from the past lives of other fruit and trees and leaves. It becomes soil, which now nurtures new life. In all of this, there is a vibrant life and beauty, even glory. Mary and I now become the soil life grows in—maybe a new seed.

Here is a favorite quote of ours from Wendell Berry's *The Autobiography of Jaber Crow*:

"None of us can see beyond death with our five senses and rational/logical minds. That limitation allows us to hold any imagination we want about our next lives."

Mary and I have chosen the best imagination, the one that has best enhanced our lives in these bodies on this earth. Why not?

In a very real way, though, this vision is far more profound than an act of imagination. It arises from all of our human experiences and the deepest source of knowing.

There are those who will feel we have made a choice only God should make, that God should take us "naturally." Our experience is that God has always come to know us more intimately through our conscious growing and has become ever more present in us as we have taken conscious responsibility for our lives. God also has guided our conscious choice in this final act. It is a calling. Medical technology has made our lives longer and more joyful. It is also used in the medical system in usual, but unspoken, ways to hasten the deaths of those who are suffering greatly with no hope of lucid recovery.

Our God cannot wait to see us, hold us to her breast. "I have only one question," she will ask, urgently. "Have you enjoyed the gift of life I gave you?" We will say,

"Yes." We are aware that our "going together" will shock many people. Others may be grateful to know that this is possible.

We have examined closely all alternative paths forward, always with a great depth of feeling and bold openness, ranging from gripping fear to deadening sadness to childlike wonder and hope. Mary cared for her mother as she suffered dementia for ten years and for her sister, Stephanie, as she suffered dementia for as many years. Her mother spent a full decade at home, the last eighteen months of it with a full time team of six caregivers. Stevie spent seven years in nursing facilities. Both lost almost complete mental capacity.

As Mary cared for them through those years, she determined that if she were struck with dementia, she did not want to live out the full ravages of the disease, losing her sense of herself, her loved ones, her life. Also, she was determined not to go into an institutional nursing facility. Of these things, she has been most certain to the end.

Knowing that my own rheumatoid arthritis, osteoarthritis, spinal stenosis, and sleep apnea would not be terminal but would bring chronic, long-term pain and suffering, I have studied methods of dying with dignity by conscious choice when my suffering became overbearing. Medicines, the people who developed them, and those passionate medical doctors, nurses, and practitioners who have cared for us, immensely extended our lives and capacity to enjoy it. Bless them all.

Yet, the time did come. It is very difficult for us humans, in the culture we have created, to accomplish a conscious, gentle, compassionate death, the kind we give to our beloved pets. Mary and I are pleased to have found great help from passionate, compassionate, and courageous people who have stood strongly for a culture and a legal structure that would allow persons to choose their own time and way of dying and get medical and personal assistance in carrying out their desires. These people see this as the next civil right, as we do. We see them as the new suffragettes. If we were younger, we would join the movement to allow and assist people to die consciously with dignity.

This "going together" has been an extremely challenging path for our family. Few longtime partners even allow themselves to consider it, even though it might feel like a wonderful culmination of their love.

Our daughters, Alex and Liz, have been in full

dialogue with us at every step of the journey, sharing all of our thoughts, wonderings, overwhelming feelings, spiritual questioning, and questing. We decided that we would move forward, step-by-step, as one and in the spirit of love rather than fear.

We would take no step until all of us were together, One, acting in love. This process has demanded immense courage and trust in God. It has also grown us deeply as a family. From all of you, our family and friends, we ask for understanding, empathy, and compassion. As Atticus Finch advised Jem and Scout in *To Kill a Mockingbird*, we hope you will "walk awhile in our shoes." From some, perhaps, we will even need forgiveness. We humbly ask for that, too.

You have played such an inextricable role in our beautiful love story, which can only be a story of relationships. "Thank you" is the most we can possibly say, and it must suffice. We hope we have been a gift of love to you as you have been to us.

"He Was Opposed, Then Supportive, and Then Inspired" *by Stephen T.*

It was five years in May since my mother used FEN to help her leave. It's taken me this long to feel okay about sharing our adventure.

On a regular Saturday, she said, "Sit down, I have something I need to tell you." I thought she had cancer. She said, "I have decided to take my own life. I've been doing research online about assisted suicide and found this place called Final Exit Network. I have sent them my medical records and am just waiting for approval."

I told her absolutely not. If she wanted to go through with this idea, I would not support her. She would have to tell me goodbye and then have Peter, her husband, call and tell me it was over.

Mom had Parkinson's, fibromyalgia, and a list of other issues. She had a constant tremor in her hand and suffered debilitating pain. She looked at me with moist eyes and said, "Do you really want me to go on living like this?" Her hands were shaking, and she was becoming unable to walk or feed herself. She said, "I can't paint anymore. I can't draw or make quilts. I am no longer able to write or

135

email. I'm becoming trapped inside this body that is in constant pain.

"I refuse to be held hostage by this disease or by the medical community just waiting to die. I refuse to become a burden on you, Ronnie, or Peter."

I felt trapped in a corner. No, I didn't want her to go on living like that, but I didn't want her to leave either. I told her I could not support her decision. I hugged her neck, and my husband and I left.

We didn't say a word on the drive back to our house. Stunned silence. Quiet disbelief. Those minutes on the drive home would be the beginning of a four-month adventure that still seems surreal. By the time we got home, I had changed my mind. I called and told her I would support whatever decision she made. I told her, if she was doing it to not be a burden, I could not support her decision, but her decision to end the pain and suffering was probably the most noble thing I had ever witnessed.

Whatever she needed me to do, I would do it with enthusiasm. From that point on, the world seemed to be different. I couldn't talk about what I was going through with anyone; I had never felt so isolated.

Mom said someone from FEN would call to talk

with me. The next day, my phone rang. It was FEN. She told me who she was, made sure she had the right person, and we talked for over an hour. Then she said, "Your mother's death day is May 25."

Out of all we were going through, everything we were trying to come to terms with, those seven words were the hardest to hear. It still rings in my head like an echo through a dark canyon. You will never be prepared to hear those words. My mother asked me to move in with them, and I did. We had three months left and she said, "I want us to be a family one more time before I leave."

It was three months of tears and laughter. It was an emotional roller coaster that I could have missed had I not been there for her. Now, I wouldn't have missed it for the world. She has twin granddaughters in Florida. I called and told them they needed to come say goodbye. "Why, what happened?" they asked. "Is she worse? Is she in the hospital? Why is it time to say goodbye?"

A thousand questions, and I had to hold the truth. I bought them airline tickets for the next weekend. They flew up and we all had a nice visit. As I was driving them back to the airport, they said, "Uncle Steve, you're overreacting. She doesn't seem any worse. Why did you make us come up here?"

Silence. I couldn't tell them. But I had an awesome idea. Both my nieces make quilts, like my mom. I asked them to make a quilt of her favorite articles of clothing. So Mom and I went through her closet, picked out clothes that she liked and shipped them to the twins. I insisted it be made quickly, and they couldn't understand why. I thought it would be something special for Peter to have once she was gone.

They mailed the quilt with one week remaining. She gave it to Peter, and it was powerful. He placed it on the back of the couch, and it's still there. I walk by it when I visit him and have memories of those clothes in that quilt. I left her house on May 24 so she and Peter could have the last night alone. She and I had breakfast the next morning. When the angel from FEN arrived, I left.

We agreed that she and Peter would be alone to say goodbye. Mom walked me to the door, obviously in pain. I said, "I love you to the moon and back, forever." She giggled and said, "That's a really long way." We hugged and she said, "You'll always be my little boy blue. Son, I hope you know that I love you and that you've always mattered to me."

I turned and walked out the door. It was over. I've never cried so hard in my life. About an hour later, Peter called and told me it really was over, and he had called the police. They were on their way and might want to speak with me, but nothing came of it.

I make it a point not to see people in their caskets. I never have wanted that image of them, lying there, burned into my memory. I walked into the chapel accidentally as Peter was saying goodbye. I almost bolted, but I saw her hands, perfectly still. No more tremors, no more pained expressions. She looked at peace for the first time in years. I touched her hand and told her, "Thank you. You done good."

The funeral director told me the casket she paid for twenty years ago was no longer available. There was a price difference, and I owed money. I asked, "How much?" He said, "$12." I laughed out loud and said, "Thanks, Mom!"

I'm sorry if this is too long or wordy. She was amazing, and I'm grateful for the opportunity to say goodbye. We had time to make amends and talk about things long buried that I never thought would come up again.

Having the opportunity that FEN provided my family gave me a new understanding of how temporary all of this really is and to not take one moment for granted. I can honestly say this adventure changed me.

The day after her funeral, I woke up around 3 a.m. At the hotel in the small town where she was buried, I took my dog outside to use the bathroom. It was pitch black, hot and balmy, like only southern nights can be. I turned on my phone and saw a Facebook post from someone I didn't know. Proverbs 31:25 was all it said. We are not religious, but I knew Proverbs was from the Bible, so I googled it: "She is clothed with strength and dignity; she can laugh at the days to come."

A chill went down my spine and a feeling of calm washed over me. I knew she had figured out a way to let me know she was okay. Another surreal moment in this adventure. It doesn't matter if anyone ever reads this. Mom, I hope you know how proud I am of you. You will always be my hero for doing what you did. A hero without a cape. An inspiration I am unable to share. I'm very, very proud to have been your son.

"A Guide Makes All the Difference" *by an Exit Guide*

I've always felt strongly that people should have the option to end their lives when its quality is no longer acceptable.

My mother's parents wanted to avoid prolonged deaths and wished to be compassionately put to sleep, like their beloved pets. My grandmother died quickly of a stroke, but my mother and I watched my cancer-ridden grandfather linger in the hospital. We pleaded with staff to somehow hurry the process. All they could do was help with pain. It took him three weeks to die, and that was just too long for him and for us.

This experience informed my mother's end of life choices, and Mom did not want a long death in a hospital or nursing home. She was in her late fifties and very healthy, so figuring out her own plan was not pressing.

When she reached her seventies, my mother had a simple little accident that pushed her to the brink of wanting to end her own life. One night, she got up to use the bathroom, and she slipped and fell. She was in pain and called an ambulance to take her to the emergency room.

An X-ray showed a fractured vertebra, so Mom was

admitted, and a surgeon repaired the crack.

She felt better for a few days. But the pain became unbearable, even worse than how she felt when she was first injured. For the next two months, she was in constant pain. She visited many doctors and had three visits to the ER, two of which ended in hospital stays. X-rays, MRIs, and different pain medications and upped dosages made no difference.

After these unsuccessful doctor's appointments, emergency room visits, and hospitalizations, my mother gave up on the medical community's ability to help her find relief. She could not live with this excruciating pain, and she wanted to end her life.

Since I had witnessed what she was going through, I was on board with her decision. We discussed self-deliverance options such as buying a gun, jumping off a bridge, swallowing all the pills and alcohol in the house, and breathing carbon monoxide in a running car with a hose on the tailpipe.

We favored the pill and alcohol method, and I called a friend with medical knowledge to see if they might have some advice. They could not help. Instead, they encouraged me to take Mom to the ER and tell the doctors we weren't leaving until they figured out why my mother was in so much pain.

At this fourth visit to the emergency room, doctors finally ordered a CT scan in the unlikely case there was something going on in the soft tissues. The results revealed an egg-sized hematoma pressing on her spine. It turned out that the surgeon had nicked a blood vessel when repairing Mom's vertebra. When the leak was cauterized and she awoke, she was already feeling better.

Through this experience, my mother's end of life values were reconfirmed and, although I continued to support her, I could not go through another wrenching and uneducated last-minute scramble. So I had a frank heart-to-heart talk with her. She needed to have a better plan.

We did a web search together, first looking up the Hemlock Society. That was no longer active, but we found links to Final Exit Network. My mother became a member and bought the book *Final Exit*, which we both read. She assembled a kit according to the 2011 handout. Though we knew about FEN exit guides, she did not want them involved. She was an independent woman and wouldn't have strangers in her home.

The instructions seemed clear, and she was confident she had a plan in place.

Years went by, and Mom's health declined. She was diagnosed with type 2 diabetes and struggled to control her unstable blood sugars. Her arthritis crippled her hands to the extent that she couldn't garden or even hold a book. She had been a volunteer for a project to clothe low-income children, but she no longer had the physical stamina required and she had to quit.

One of the final straws was developing cognitive decline and having her bridge partners ask her to leave their foursome because she was making so many mistakes. My mother prided herself on her intelligence, independence, and ability to be of service. At seventy-nine, she decided she had lived a long and wonderful life, but now this limited existence was intolerable and she was ready to leave.

In the meantime, California's End of Life Option Act (June 2016) had just gone into effect. We carefully studied its requirements. I doubted Mom would qualify since she did not have an end-stage disease with a six-month or less life expectancy. She was confident her personal doctor of more than thirty years would support her claim that old age was a terminal illness.

When we went to visit him, he explained that my mother's request was his first, and he agreed to look into it. A week later, he told her that she wasn't eligible for that life-ending option. She was furious and felt betrayed, but I reminded her she had her Final Exit Network backup plan and everything was still in her closet.

Suddenly this was real, not a hypothetical what-if. I started feeling sick to my stomach. Is she truly going to go through with it? Is she really ready? Am I? What would happen if this didn't work and she ended up in a coma? I wouldn't put a pillow over my mother's face. And I didn't want to be directly involved with her death. I was the single parent of a teenager. I didn't know what the laws were regarding assisting a suicide, and we were both unwilling for me to go to jail.

I strongly encouraged Mom to apply to Final Exit Network's exit guide program, but since she had been rejected by her beloved doctor, she was worried she wouldn't be accepted. So she was on her own.

We reviewed the self-deliverance instructions several more times. We were both clear that I would not be with her, but I did watch as my mom practiced.

She chose a date. I visited the night before her planned exit and we said our goodbyes.

The plan was that I would be the "discovery" person. Mother would exit in the morning, and I would phone her in the afternoon like a normal check-in. Then, when she didn't pick up after several calls, I would go to her and be "surprised" to find her body.

Instead, I received a call in the morning: "I don't know what happened. It didn't work," Mom said.

I won't go into detail, but it took her three more attempts over ten days. She eventually reverted to non-FEN approaches before she finally died.

That week and a half was probably the most nerve-wracking time in both our lives. While we were scared and unsure about the different methods she was trying, we also managed to joke a little. When the first try failed, we went out for her second "last meal." Mom had diabetes and she decided to order a milkshake, saying, "Maybe this will kill me!"

Before what became her final attempt, we agreed I wouldn't stop by her house for a day and a half in case it took her that long to die. When she didn't answer my call thirty-six hours later, I drove to her home, and she had died.

She actually looked peaceful, so that was a huge relief.

While waiting for paramedics to arrive, I knew they would take her body, so I took some photos in case my family wanted to see (and they did).

I am so grateful my mother finally found the death she wanted, but the process was terrifying. After my son went to college and I retired, I decided to volunteer with FEN. I didn't want others or their families to go through what we experienced.

I started first as an interviewer, then an associate guide, and currently I'm a senior guide. From my training, I now know what went wrong with my mother's first two attempts—user errors and obsolete instructions. She didn't know the helium balloon tanks were being diluted with oxygen.

If she'd been open to having trained guides provide her with updated self-deliverance education, I am 100 percent convinced she would have died quickly the first time.

I wish there was an easy pill we could take when we felt ready, but this doesn't exist.

If you or a loved one are looking at end of life options, especially if you don't have access to Medical Aid in Dying where you live, I strongly encourage you to find out more about FEN's exit guide program. As a guide, I have witnessed clients and their loved ones experience peace of mind knowing there is a reliable plan in place.

My mother and I did not have this comfort, but now I am making it up to both of us by educating others who seek end of life options.

"Cruel Death" *by Jay Niver*

Barbara M. lived a nightmare. Because of it, North Carolina is three steps closer to gaining right to die legislation. It's a case of good coming from bad, but Barbara wishes there had been no chance for a silver lining.

Her father, ninety-three-year-old Joe, suffered a horrific death against his wishes in 2013 after taking every conceivable step to die peacefully in his Pottsville, Pennsylvania, home. Barbara and her family endured a bogus prosecution for her alleged assistance in a suicide. It made national news, including a *60 Minutes* segment with Anderson Cooper.

Ed Tiryakian, a retired investment banker with a law degree, was watching in his North Carolina home. "I was so shocked and moved and horrified by this story," he recalls. "This World War II veteran made it absolutely clear what he wanted for the end of his life, and that poor man died fearful for his daughter's arrest. I was so angry at what she went through."

Barbara had handed her father a small vial of prescribed morphine at his request, and he drank it shortly before a home hospice nurse arrived. Then Joe's loving daughter made the tragic mistake of mentioning it to the nurse. She called her superiors, who summoned police and EMS.

When they arrived, Joe was forcibly taken to an emergency room. Barbara was arrested and taken into custody. Joe died a horrible hospital death after five days of lifesaving measures he never wanted. Charges against her were dropped after a year of excruciating torment and almost universal public outcry against the sham prosecution that turned her life upside down.

"The collateral effects have been pretty severe," she says. "It's been very tough emotionally, and I don't think I'll ever get over that." More than six years after her ordeal (legally) ended, and after telling it countless times in speaking engagements and interviews, she still finds it difficult to recount. "I had different plans for my life. I will never work as a nurse again. It does a number on you," she says. "I had an opportunity to bring injustices into the public consciousness, and I'm very glad I did that. But, boy, I wish this had never happened, especially for my father. He was tortured at the end."

Absolutely tortured. And he did everything he was supposed to do to prevent that from happening.

"This really riles me up, that you can go through all these steps, have the conversations about your values and your goals for care, and it's written down! Then, to have people in positions of power come and say, 'Nope, that's not gonna happen,'" Barbara added.

Tiryakian was also riled up. He formed a nonprofit advocacy group, Dying Right NC, to pursue Medical Aid in Dying legislation in his native state.

Bills have been filed in three legislative sessions, and the last one in 2019 boasted bipartisan sponsorship for the first time. In notoriously "red state" North Carolina, House Bill 879 (End of Life Option Act) was co-sponsored by two powerful Republicans as well as the usual Democrats. Tiryakian is a dynamo who—before COVID-19—spent as much time in the North Carolina statehouse as some elected representatives. He pretty much funds the cause out of his own pocket.

"I would not be doing what I am right now had it not been for Barbara's story," he says. "I decided that the laws and practices that had tripped her up cannot stand anywhere in America—and I set out to make sure that, at least in North Carolina, we'd pass a law making her nightmare something never repeated."

Barbara didn't seek the spotlight when she was thrust into the maelstrom surrounding her father's death. The fact was, she was a reserved, private person and ER nurse. She was also a devoted, adoring daughter who wanted to help her father achieve the exit he planned. "I totally get that a lot of these situations are not black and white," Barbara said, "but my goodness! When you have people not even pretending to honor a document, it should scare everybody."

She emerged from the experience focused on three critical issues: hospice care, laws against assisted suicide, and the criminal justice system. She was abused by all three and wanted to spread the word. Barbara's father-daughter family ordeal was triggered when she mentioned morphine to the hospice nurse. In retrospect, is she glad it may spur reform?

She replied without hesitation. "I wish I had never said anything that day." The case against her eventually disclosed substantial hospice failure on many levels. Her own subsequent sleuthing revealed that all hospices are not created equal. "My biggest regret is that I didn't do more to research hospice care," she confessed. "There's a heightened awareness about criminal justice issues everywhere now. Things have been exposed about how prosecutors and police scam the system."

Since joining the right to die cause—albeit regretfully—she has added a fourth plank to her reform platform: "The politics around how people are allowed to die . . . This journey has been a real education for me, especially when you talk about legislation being passed," she explained.

Barbara testifies before state lawmakers who are considering MAID. She's had some eye-opening revelations, particularly in Connecticut. "I was supposed to be eighteenth to speak," she recalled. "Everybody was given three minutes to say their piece.

"The hearing started at 9 a.m., and I finally got to testify at 9:30 p.m. that night. They were basically filibustering. When people opposed to aid in dying spoke, committee members who agreed with them would ask question after question. A three-minute testimony got drawn out to sometimes sixty minutes. The tactic is to stop a bill before it ever gets out of committee, if it even gets that far."

"Relief from Hospice" *by Jay Niver*

When doctors found inoperable stage four cancer in Bob Bruno, he was sent that same day to the only hospice in Sarasota, Florida. His wife, Esta Asteroff, suspected there could be trouble. Her aunt had a horribly painful time there in 2008.

"Some days, she was screaming so badly with horrific hallucinations," she recalls. "I kept begging them to give her more morphine. It was heart-wrenching to watch."

Now, twelve years later, would it be any different for her husband? "He was in such distress and agitation and pain and discomfort, and every day was a fight with the doctor for additional medication," Esta says.

It got worse on day five. "From 11 p.m. until 1:30 a.m., he was in such dire straits and the nurse gave him everything she could. Then she looked at me and said, 'He's transitioning,' which is a very strange euphemism for dying. He was in agony and calling out and thrashing around and I said, 'Can't you help him?' She claimed not. Later, I found out that was simply not true. She could have called the on-call physician to get additional medication for Bob. She chose not to do so and lied to me."

What happened next, says Esta, was unconscionable. "The nurse said, 'Maybe you'd like to move your husband to another facility?' I said, 'I would love to move my husband, but there's none other in Sarasota.'" Bob was not transitioning. His ordeal would last another five days, and things finally improved after an indirect FEN intervention.

Esta, who was a longtime FEN member, had a college friend she had known for decades, a woman who had since worked years with FEN. Esta reached out to her friend, who put her in touch with FEN's attorney.

Sometimes called a proxy or agent, a surrogate is someone assigned through an advance directive to make decisions for a dying person who is no longer competent to do so. The irony of Esta's case is that she was the surrogate for both Bob and her aunt—and it made no difference to the hospice. "We had all the paperwork done in 2018," Esta explains. "We did wills, advance directives, health care proxies. Everything was in order.

"[The attorney] told me I had the right to demand that Bob get all the pain medication he was legally entitled to, which was far more than they were giving him. If it was, like, from one to one hundred, we were still at seven. I had a right to insist on that and they had an obligation to do it. They simply did not want to provide morphine to him."

On day six, armed with legal encouragement, Esta confronted the doctor and "it seemed to escalate them," she recalls. "I think they got a little scared. They knew that I knew I had rights." Bob's meds were increased "to where he was at least peaceful."

Esta's opinion of the Sarasota hospice sank even further when she learned that it had stopped another hospice from setting up there in 2018. She says the number of beds should not determine need if care is substandard and there is "no choice for the public." She believes that a profit motive can interfere with altruistic ones, and data seems to support that. In the 1980s and 1990s, nonprofits provided virtually all US hospice care. By 2016, more than two-thirds were for profit, and only twenty percent were nonprofit.

Since then, every new hospice has been profit oriented. The money is good. The profit margin of for-profit hospices is more than four times higher than for nonprofits struggling to stay afloat.

"Hospices make more money from patients who live a long time than those who die quickly," The

Huffington Post reported. "That incentivizes [them] to cherry-pick the healthiest patients to boost gains." HuffPost added: "In dozens of lawsuits, federal prosecutors have accused hospice companies, including almost all of the largest players, of billing fraud, alleging they enrolled patients who didn't qualify and signed them up for extra expensive levels of care."

In 2017, for-profits discharged more than one in five of their patients alive. More than 460 companies discharged more than half of their "customers" before they died. For her husband Bob, Esta believes there was also a cultural stance aligned against them in Sarasota. "I think they have a philosophy where all life, no matter how bad, is to be lived as long as you can possibly live it," she says.

"Peace and Love—Neta's Story" *by Dick M.*

Neta was a Florida resident I met during my speaking tour. She requested some personal time before a meeting near her home, as she wished to learn what Final Exit Network offered to members and supporters. For years, Neta belonged to the Hemlock Society and learned it no longer had a support program for those wishing to plan their end of life choice. That led her to join FEN, and Neta revealed by email that she would be changing her targeted support to us.

Two years later, I was told that Neta had applied for exit guide services. After she was approved, Jim, a guide who lived in Florida, was assigned, and Neta asked that I be on her guide team. I assured her I would be honored, but I hoped it would be some time before she felt the time was right. Meanwhile, she said she found such peace of mind to know FEN would support her when she chose.

Neta embarked on a crusade to publicly try to improve social issues. She wrote four books, part memoir and part issue-oriented, like the right of patients to control how and when they die. One of her books was a memoir of an around-the-world cruise she took, which she said was a tribute to her husband, John, with whom she had enjoyed a similar cruise many years earlier. For another book, she asked me and others to contribute about dying and how one should have the right to control that important part of life. We often had email conversations about it.

Neta concluded all of our communications with "Peace and Love."

Fast forward to 2020. Neta was working on another book and, apparently, still able to enjoy her mostly homebound activities. On the last day of January, she was admitted to the hospital in severe pain due to a compression fracture of a vertebra, secondary to her long history of osteoporosis. She immediately stated, "This is it!"

Calling from her hospital bed, Neta said physicians had warned her for years that multiple bone compressions might occur. The pain was so intense, she didn't wish to risk any more, and she feared a nursing home would be required to care for her. She asked to set a time for her long-standing plan to exit. She did, however, accept the advice of her orthopedic doctor, who suggested the pain could be controlled by an injection of stem cells into her vertebrae. This procedure was a minimally invasive approach with reportedly excellent results.

A day after the treatment, Neta told me she was much more comfortable and would be discharged soon. As soon as Neta returned home, she started planning an exit date. She had two good friends who would be with her when she died, and she had all the needed apparatuses to accomplish that.

Unfortunately, her guide died before Neta arranged her exit. She had contacted FEN president and senior guide Brian Ruder, with whom she had connected after he called to acknowledge her annual FEN donation. He agreed to be on her guide team when she wished to proceed. With Neta, Brian and I agreed to a date in the last week of February, and Neta organized her friends for that time. Brian and I arranged our travel plans so we could arrive about the same time, and we booked hotel rooms.

Late in the afternoon, while I packed for my flight east, Brian called to say that Neta had again been admitted to the hospital. Due to the spinal injury, complete bed rest had been ordered to avoid other vertebral compressions. Her usual activities before the fracture included being freely up and around and having a personal trainer provide her with supervised exercises two or three times weekly. Being static in bed created another problem; her lower legs

160

swelled and caused increasing pain.

A doctor who made home visits prescribed pain medication and antibiotics. When symptoms became more severe, Neta was hospitalized for intravenous antibiotics and pain relief. Her panicked call to Brian stalled our travel plans. I received daily calls from Neta; one of her private nurses described continuation of her leg symptoms and sent photographs. Pain medication was helping some, but Neta became more insistent that she be at home for her exit. She asked Brian and me to be with her soon after she returned home.

A consulting vascular specialist visited Neta in the hospital. He discontinued the antibiotic infusions and ordered compression stockings. In early March, Neta finally returned home. As this cavalcade of the unexpected unfolded, another was added. On March 11, state and federal leaders realized that COVID-19 had become a pandemic as predicted by the World Health Organization. In my home state of California, the governor ordered all residents to isolate themselves at home, essentially shutting everything down. Airlines were reducing flights. East coast states soon had increasing numbers of virus-stricken patients, and hospitals reported overwhelmed emergency rooms and intensive care units.

Neta resumed plans to proceed with her exit. She felt it could be weeks before she had the strength to act, and a date was set for late March. Then another hurdle arose: Neta's condo complex of mostly senior residents was at too much risk to permit visitors. So much for seeing her, let alone attending her exit.

At this point, Neta and I talked daily, and she somehow made great efforts still to proceed, without any seemingly possible road ahead. It was then that we discussed if she would consider VSED—Voluntarily Stopping Eating and Drinking—and ask for home hospice care.

With no hope of us traveling to her, Neta decided on VSED at the end of March. After two days, hospice accepted her for care at home. I called Neta daily. Occasionally, a nurse would answer to say she was resting but would call back. Neta was able to obtain morphine for pain if she complained that lesser medication didn't help. Thus, she had some peaceful sleep and, with five days of fasting, her voice became very weak. Still, in early April, Neta was more able to speak and I asked her about her intake of fluids. She said one of the private nurses gave her

sweetened tea in small quantities, plus sips of water. Neta
put the nurse on the phone and she told me that she
understood what Neta wanted, but her agency's supervisor
did not approve.

When talking with Neta, I explained again that even
small amounts of liquid could delay her death. By April 9,
Neta again sounded extremely weak. She said she was
having a little pain and sleeping a lot.

Once more, I told her how disappointed Brian and I
were at not being able to be with her. Neta said how much
she wished that could have been possible, and she
appreciated that we had tried. That afternoon, as usual, she
ended the call as she had ended emails for years: "Peace
and Love."

It was the last time we talked. My daily calls went
unanswered. I learned later that fluids were still being
given. Neta's closest friend alerted the estate administrator,
who intervened with a threat of legal action to finally get
Neta's dying wish fulfilled.

Health crises and a pandemic thwarted her end of
life plans, but not Neta's spirit and determination. Months
earlier, anticipating death, she penned the following words

excerpted from a message to her friends and family to be delivered after her passing:

'To All My Angels'
I am homebound now
On the greatest journey of them all . . .
Earth time must not confine me
As I must answer the call of eternal time . . .

"It's Time" *by Janet Grossman*

Perhaps the greatest single reason I got involved with FEN is because I don't believe that any true love story like my parents' should end in fear, secrecy, and pain.

My parents were free thinkers and I was reared to be one too. Of course, I didn't realize until later in my life how different they were from their families of origin, and that I was from my classmates. I can remember multiple dinner table conversations starting when I was in elementary school when my parents would talk about signs of dementia and say that if they ever showed any such signs, I should tell them immediately so they could kill themselves before it got so bad that they couldn't do it. I never thought this was an imminent danger, but something that might happen many years in the future. They told me about my father's father, who had developed dementia at an extremely young age, became unable to hold a job, and spent the last eighteen months of his life in an institution, wearing diapers, being spoon-fed, and communicating only in grunts. He died at age sixty, just before I was born.

My parents joined the Hemlock Society at its
inception, and were members of state Death with Dignity
groups and Compassion & Choices. They had read *Final
Exit*, and my dad had some of the equipment for the helium
method of self-deliverance. The big shock to my father and
me was that when my mother developed vascular dementia
due to ministrokes of which nobody had been aware, then
Alzheimer's disease along with it, she never understood
that she had it. My dad and I both told her, and we saw
their family doctor together to discuss our concerns. Then
she was referred to a neurologist who also told her what she
had. Eventually she was spending half days at the adult
day-care center, but she thought she worked there full-time.
At least that gave my dad a chance to do shopping, attend a
caregivers' support group, and generally take care of
himself. He would frequently turn up at my office since it
was nearby, and if I wasn't with a client, we'd talk about
how things were going and his plans to end their lives.
They had always made clear that they would never go into
assisted living, and by the time they were living
independently in an "aging in place" community, it was
clear that would soon be their only option, though she

might need to be in a memory care unit, which neither of them would agree to.

My mother ended up in the ER several times with dehydration, as she kept ignoring the cups of water we left all around their unit. I finally asked if she was choosing to end her life by dehydration, to which she replied that of course she wasn't. I told her we were going to keep reminding her to drink, but my dad came up with an idea that actually worked. Although my parents weren't heavy or daily drinkers, my mom had always liked gin and tonic. He started making two of them for her each evening, but leaving out the gin, and she enjoyed her tonic water with ice and lime, never giving any indication that anything was missing. No more trips to the ER for dehydration!

My parents had always done a lot of volunteer work, particularly doing stream monitoring with the Sierra Club. But my mother was fired from this duty when she became unable to do the required measurements, so my dad asked me to help come up with something they could do every Saturday morning so she wouldn't just lie on the couch in a fetal position in her nightclothes. Monday through Friday, she went to the adult day-care center, and

Sunday they went to the Unitarian Universalist fellowship, of which they had been founding members, so she already got up and dressed those days. My father didn't like any of my suggestions, but called me one day saying he had decided they'd walk dogs for the Humane Society on Saturday mornings. My reply was, "But you don't like dogs!" He said, "Exactly, so we won't get emotionally attached and want to bring one home with us!" That actually worked really well, as my dad held the leashes and my mom carried the dog treats.

Then my father was diagnosed with congestive heart failure, and he said to me, "I no longer have the energy to take care of myself, much less both of us, so it's time." He insisted the only sure method would be for him to shoot my mother and then himself. I argued with this quite a bit, but he shot down all my ideas too. Finally, he set the day and time, making sure it would be dark so nobody would see them in the parking lot he'd chosen, but early enough for the police to come notify me before it was too late on a work night for me. About half an hour after the planned time, he called to say it didn't happen because my mother didn't agree, and asking my partner to buy him a pair of jeans at a thrift store the next day, as he'd donated all his clothes already.

Two days later, he called and said my mother had agreed, so the plan was on for that night. He had written something for me to email to various people after their deaths, and since my mom had been a technical writer and editor, he had her review it. She did, and he reported that she had said, "You're right. It's time." All went as he had planned it, except that the police didn't come to tell me about it until 11:00 that night, though of course I didn't go to work the next day anyway. I called my supervisor about 11:30 and told her what had happened. She said, "You know, the company gives employees three days off for the death of an immediate family member." I'm still surprised that I had the presence of mind to reply, "I just lost two, so do I get six days off?" The answer was yes. The other exception was that although my father died immediately, my mother didn't. He would have been devastated to know that she lived long enough to be airlifted to the nearest trauma center, where she died about 12 hours after the gunshot.

A few months after their deaths, I learned of Final Exit Network and promptly became a lifetime member. I don't believe my parents were aware of FEN, but even if they had been, my mother wouldn't have qualified for Exit Guide Services, as no one would have said she was mentally competent. I was thrilled when I learned of an upcoming volunteer training a few years after that, and have played multiple roles since my training. Although most of my working career was in the nonprofit world, my volunteer work with FEN is the most meaningful job I've ever done.

"Death Was Her 'Last Frontier'" *by Althea Halchuck*

The following piece chronicles the experience of two FEN clients whose names have been changed for privacy. Althea Halchuck, FEN's surrogate consultant, wrote this piece with their permission in order to share their story.

*****

Carol to Althea: My best friend of fifty years, Evelyn, is a patient in a large Boston teaching hospital. Doctors are not respecting her, or me as her health care power of attorney, or following her advance directives. I need your help.

Evelyn has nearly a dozen severe comorbidities and has endured continual pain for the last fifteen months while recuperating from three surgeries. She is very clear about her end of life wishes, which we've discussed many times —no more surgeries, no intubation, no artificial feeding, no resuscitation.

Several days ago, after a 911 call, Evelyn was transferred to her treating surgeon. I was told she had consented to surgery, requiring intubation. During an eight-hour operation, they discovered a blood clot and suspected part of her bowel might have died. She was in critical condition, and the prognosis was hour by hour. On day two, she was extubated; on day three, she was up doing physical therapy, but in lots of pain.

We immediately updated her DNR and POLST (Physician Orders for Life Sustaining Treatment), indicating comfort-focused treatment only and no resuscitation.

She didn't stabilize, the pain increased, and the doctors decided—without asking for consent—to withdraw food and oral meds to help her bowel recover, requiring a feeding tube. Then they installed a PICC (peripherally inserted central catheter) line to give her nutrition and medication.

They claimed Evelyn was on the road to recovery. Conflicted as I was, I didn't want to withdraw treatment, which would mean certain death. Two weeks later, the attending surgeon called to say immediate surgery was needed to uncover the cause of her pain, suspecting a dead bowel. She claimed if Evelyn didn't have this surgery, she would likely suffer a long, slow death from sepsis. Although she had consented to the surgery, doctors weren't sure she understood, and they wanted my consent. Despite my better judgment, I agreed.

Carol continues relating the experience:

An hour later, her nurse called and said when they came to take her to surgery, she didn't want to go and was kicking and screaming, but they took her anyway. I immediately called the OR to withdraw consent. Realizing I needed FEN's help, I promptly placed a call requesting Althea's help. Within an hour, on a conference call, the treating and attending surgeons pleaded with me to consent to two possible operations.

The treating surgeon said this was a fixable condition and they could go in and "take a look-see." The other surgeon said, "I can't agree." But the treating surgeon refused to take no for an answer and proceeded to discuss procedures and argue. He applied additional pressure, saying he would not give her huge doses of pain meds to let her die or put her in hospice.

Finally, the anesthesiologist said, "I know her. I've participated in her last three surgeries, and she wouldn't want this." With that, I firmly cut off discussions with their promise to transfer Evelyn to comfort care—with no surgery.

Later that evening, the attending surgeon called to say, "I think we made the right decision." I was confused, as she had advocated for surgery until the last minute. The following morning, she called to say the treating surgeon had talked Evelyn into an operation, but the attending physician didn't think she was competent to decide. I demanded a call from the treating surgeon.

While Althea listened in, the doctor again pleaded for surgery. He had an answer for every question and objection I had about bad outcomes. He was not going to transfer her to hospice, period. I told him firmly yet again: Evelyn's wish was for no treatment. He finally agreed to call in palliative care.

I spoke with the palliative care team, and it was a complete and complex phone call with no pushback. They reiterated that I had full control to make the decisions. They were totally supportive to immediately withdraw antibiotics and feeding, confirming what Althea had said about my right to decide things. Still, after all this, palliative care had to wrest control from the treating surgeon because he claimed, "The team was still debating whether to put Evelyn with hospice."

When I walked into her room the next day, she said, "Thank goodness you're here; I can go now." Finally, after many weeks, I enrolled her in hospice. I had to advocate every step of the way to ensure she was receiving adequate pain medication.

After six days in hospice, she peacefully passed.

*****

Althea adds context: Carol called me midway through her struggles on behalf of Evelyn. She encountered doctors who refused to listen, had their own agendas, or gave conflicting information. The treating surgeon's goal was to get her well enough for "one last Alaska dogsled adventure." He pushed treatments and surgery on a dying woman rather than refer her to hospice. Another issue: Evelyn was in and out of mental capacity, not realizing the consequences of surgery or understanding doctors' requests.

After reviewing Evelyn's end of life documents, I determined Carol was her HC-POA and had every right to make her medical choices. I had suggested Carol reach out to palliative care for a consultation, and contact the Ethics Committee. Carol was a strong and intelligent advocate being ignored and pushed and pulled in every direction. She was also in the midst of anticipatory grief over her failing friend. At various points, Carol was angry,

frustrated, confused, and conflicted. After she spoke to
palliative care, Carol wrote: "The biggest compliment I
can give is that speaking with palliative care felt almost as
good as speaking with you. You have helped me immensely.
I thought I was a knowledgeable advocate, but I never
imagined there would be so many roadblocks. As the
journey unfolded, a nurse and two doctors remarked,
'When it's my time, I hope I have an advocate like you.'
Knowing you were there helped infuse me with strength. I
am so very grateful . . . "

"My Story" *by Myriam Coppens*

It all began when I was in nursing school at the University of Louvain, Belgium, in 1962. The hospital was under the direction of Catholic nuns. At one point when I worked on a cancer ward, a particular patient would continuously scream for pain medication and ask to die. There was nothing I could do. In those days, pain and suffering was seen as a way to save souls. This was beyond my understanding!

Years later, I was approached by a former patient while shopping at Nordstrom. She was struggling with metastatic breast cancer and wanted me to help her end her life. I was totally at a loss and ill-prepared to respond, although supportive and understanding of her wishes. Again, there was nothing I could do!

When this happened to me for the third time, in 1985, a former patient asked me to be his advocate when the time came for his suffering to end from years of diabetes and multiple amputations. This time I said yes! I got the call that he was in the hospital with peritonitis and was in a tremendous amount of pain. He had been told by his physician he would need an additional amputation. This brave, proud, independent man repeatedly asked his doctors and nurses, "How much longer?"

A morphine drip was clearly not touching his grievous discomfort, and the physician indicated that he was likely to live for at least another week in this state. After multiple phone conversations, she reluctantly agreed to increase his morphine drip. He died later that night with his significant other by his side.

I met Derek Humphry and decided to open the Hemlock Society chapter of Portland in 1989. I took all the calls until the chapter closed in 1997, when the right to die law passed in Oregon.

With the law passed, I was no longer involved in this amazing work, as there was little need in my community. In 2008, I discovered FEN's mission and reconnected with this inspiring work. I met a great group of volunteers, pioneers of what is FEN today. Working with patients and their families has been deeply rewarding and a privilege.

NOTES OF APPRECIATION FROM CLIENTS

"Words Cannot Express" *by Anonymous*

Words simply cannot express how grateful Joe and I are for your help at such a monumental moment in our lives. You are the angels that we have been praying for. Thank you for making this moment a beautiful experience for us. This is the last moment we will have on this earth together. You have given Joe his dignity, and you have given us a calmness and allowed us to do this together on our own terms in the privacy of our home, where we have lived together for over twenty years.

You will now have another angel looking over you, and I have now become a permanent member of your organization. I will continue to support what you do through donations. What you do is so crucial to people like me. I will NEVER forget what you have given us. Thank you from the bottom of my heart.

"Blessed by the Universe" *by Anonymous*

Dear [Coordinator],

I wanted to write my thanks to you before time runs out. You've smoothed the way for me greatly and my guide is following suit. I feel very blessed by the universe! Something I want to capture and share with you and FEN is the great sense of peace I feel now that I'm closing whole areas of what has been a fulfilling life. It feels right to be closing out belongings and past accomplishments, to linger over pictures before I discard them, and to be able to take time while I'm still well enough to rest in my gratitude for everyone and everything. Under ordinary circumstances, I think one would be too ill or stressed to have this luxury of time for reflection and appreciation.

I'm so glad I started the process back in the fall, as my tumor is relentless in its progression, and I emphasize how important starting is. Once begun, you in the organization have made it all move forward so smoothly. I thank you deeply for your commitment, kindness, and caring, and I wish you a long and happy life.

EDITOR'S NOTE

Knowing the importance of personal stories to help explain who Final Exit Network is and what FEN does, it occurred to me that a collection of these pieces might be valuable to the FEN community and beyond. As a retired librarian, I envisioned a physical book that could be made available in libraries and bookstores, at public programs, passed among friends and family members to commemorate, celebrate, and explain FEN's unique role in the right to die movement.

I hope you've enjoyed this never-before-seen portrait of FEN's committed and compassionate volunteers and grateful clientele.

We are grateful to all who participated in this project, and hope that it helps to make a broader audience aware of the availability of FEN's support services. For more information, go to www.finalexitnetwork.org.

-Jim Van Buskirk
Anthology Editor

ACKNOWLEDGMENTS

Thanks to FEN Board President Brian Ruder and Executive Director Mary Ewert for their early support in assembling the project team.

Most of these essays were originally published in a slightly different form in Final Exit Network's quarterly magazine, and we appreciate all of FEN's magazine editors who have served the organization throughout the years. Contributors' names have been changed where necessary to protect the identities of those involved. While many of these submissions were not written by professionals, their authenticity contributes mightily to their power and importance.